LAURA ASHLEY

THE *colour* BOOK

LAURA ASHLEY

THE *colour* BOOK

USING COLOUR TO DECORATE YOUR HOME

SUSAN BERRY

Special Photography by David Brittain

EBURY PRESS
LONDON

First published in 1995

1 3 5 7 9 10 8 6 4 2

Text copyright © Laura Ashley 1995
Photography copyright © David Brittain 1995 unless otherwise stated; see copyright owners
on page 206

First published in the United Kingdom in 1995 by Ebury Press
Random House, 20 Vauxhall Bridge Road, London SW1V 2SA

Random House Australia (Pty) Limited
20 Alfred Street, Milsons Point, Sydney.
New South Wales 2061, Australia

Random House New Zealand Limited
18 Poland Road, Glenfield
Auckland 10, New Zealand

Random House South Africa (Pty) Limited
PO Box 337, Bergvlei, South Africa

Random House UK Limited Reg. No. 954009
British Library Cataloguing in Publication Data. A catalogue record for this book is
available from the British Library.

Project Editor: Jane Struthers
Pages 74–5, 96–7, 104–5, 156–7, 166–7 and 196–7 by Alison Wormleighton
Designed by Christine Wood
Special photography by David Brittain
Styling by Jacky Boase
Picture research by Emily Hedges

ISBN 0 09 180723 9

Colour separations produced in Italy by Colorlito Rigogliosi, Milan
Printed and bound in Great Britain by Butler & Tanner Ltd, Frome and London

Papers used by Ebury Press are natural recyclable products made from wood grown in
sustainable forests.

Contents

Introduction

In some respects, the use of colour has come full circle since Laura Ashley's initial success in home furnishings in the late 1970s. The image that most people conjure up when they think of traditional Laura Ashley decoration is of a romantic country bedroom decorated in small floral prints. These were dress prints used in the same way that the French use toile de Jouy – using a blue print on a white ground for the walls, and a white print on a blue ground for the curtains – and they gave Laura Ashley its distinctive country look. This was essentially monochrome decorating, which was very popular in the 1970s, and has since seen a return to fashion in the 1990s.

Just as the Arts and Crafts movement of the nineteenth century had looked to natural colours rather than synthetic ones, Laura Ashley's original colour palette reflected the naturalness of the country, and the use of natural dyes. The range featured browns such as oak and saddle, earth colours, terracotta and cream, navy and burgundy, muted mid-tone colours such as smoke and plum and, for a more masculine look, dark green on white. These colours worked well with the warm tones of stripped pine, terracotta tiles, the simplicity of brass beds on bare floorboards, rag rugs and a nostalgia for an idealized life in the country before the advent of the modern age.

These colours were designed to work on their own in decorating, although there were some natural colour groupings, such as the browns with terracotta, and smoke with plum. There were no rules, particularly as to which colours suited which rooms, so navy was as acceptable in a bedroom as plum and rose. Other colours were introduced, and a bright colour palette reflected contemporary decorating trends. Poppy red, apple green, bright yellow mustard and china blue were all easy and bright to use in kitchens and bathrooms, and also in children's bedrooms.

In the early 1980s, soft pastel colours – including pale pink, rose, sapphire blue and apricot – were introduced and remained extremely popular throughout the decade. The prints themselves were developed to include more colours, and the colour palette became much more sophisticated. Combinations of colours were important in creating different looks – a particularly crucial point was varying the shade of green used in the foliage of floral prints so that it would work with the main colour. Rose and sapphire were linked with moss green, smoke and plum with a dirty sage, and a pale aquamarine was combined with a rich apricot.

At first, the decorating story was simple, but by the second half of the 1980s, the chintz

This Louis XVI bedroom in a French chateau was decorated by Laura Ashley in 1984 to introduce a new blue, called kingfisher, to the collection. The fabric is called Antoinette and the design was based on a French eighteenth-century silk print.

room had introduced riots of colour as fabrics reflected the herbaceous borders in country house gardens. The romantic cottage had turned into the romantic country house. The pastels developed into many more varieties of shades and tones. Navy, burgundy and dark green replaced brown at the darker end of the colour spectrum, but were now used with a sand background, rather than white, for a more sophisticated, traditional look redolent of country house libraries.

At the end of the 1980s, cowslip yellow became very fashionable. After the popularity of pastel colours earlier in the decade, there was a need for something brighter, but not primary, and cowslip yellow was perfect. Two particularly popular designs were Laura Ashley's Lyme Regis wallpaper in cowslip, and the Alba Roses chintz, which is a striking floral bouquet spaced on a white ground, and on a larger scale than many of the earlier designs. Many other designs in cowslip followed, the most notable of which was Sweet Pea, which combined various tones of cowslip and sapphire blue in a stunning, sunny, floral print which was particularly popular.

Many colours have been introduced for specific purposes – a warmer red, a clearer blue, heath green which is more yellow than the blue-green jade, and different shades of white for varying grounds to fabrics and wallpapers. Colours have also been introduced for individual collections, such as jade, crimson and ivory for the Chinoiserie Collection, and midnight blue and gold for a theme based on Venetian and Renaissance designs.

More recently, colour versus non-colour has become a big design issue. Taupe, which was introduced as a background colour in some multi-coloured floral prints in the 1980s, took over as the basis for a whole range of neutral colours that have become the vogue in the early 1990s. Alongside this has been the faded florals look, where all the tones of differing colours have been equalized to give the effect of having been aged by the sun. This makes them look instantly at home in a decorating scheme. In contrast, the bright, rich colours of the hot climates from India to the South of France are evident – chambray blue and plaster pink, ochres and russets, deep pinks and rich blues.

In general, people's ideas about decorating have become much more adventurous and knowledgeable since Laura Ashley was first in business, and colour has emerged as the most important element in home design for the 1990s. This book will help you to understand colour better, appreciate the subtleties of particular hues and enhance your decorating skills in a variety of different ways.

ABOVE *This new print in cowslip, called Paeony, was launched in 1992. Cowslip is still a popular decorating colour.*

BELOW *This kitchen shows the Kitchen Garden print in plaster pink, a marvellous 1990s colour.*

CHAPTER 1

living with colour

It is surprising how many people, who are fairly confident and assured about their taste, lose all that confidence when trying to mix and match colours. Instead of following their instincts, and deciding what appeals to them and what they enjoy looking at, they become indecisive and ill-at-ease. In fact, there are no fixed rules when it comes to colour and it pays to forget all those old adages you learned at your grandmother's knee – that blue and green should never be seen, and that red and orange clash. So much depends not only on colour, but on shape, on texture, the amount of colour used, and the amount and type of light in the room too.

When it comes to interior decorating, the sheer scale on which the colour is seen can be extremely confusing. What looks good in a paint sample not much bigger than the bristles on a paintbrush might be too dominating or too insipid when spread over an enormous expanse of wall. Equally, colours that do not go together when seen in small amounts held close together, can blend and harmonize surprisingly well when they are some distance from each other in a large room. Using a patterned fabric that contains the two colours you wish to use can be a good way to unify the decorating scheme if you are unsure of the effect they will create on their own.

If you are used to colour-matching clothes, where the amounts of colour and fabric involved are relatively small, it may come as a great surprise that you have a lot more scope as an interior decorator. It is not as important to match the exact tone or shade of a colour in a room as it is in an outfit, although you must be aware of the long-distance effect. People do not walk into a room and examine a cushion from a distance of about 60 cm (2 feet), as you may do when choosing one in a department store. They notice, or fail to notice, the effect from about 3.1 metres (10 feet), and the object will be surrounded by other colours, surfaces and textures, all of which may harmonize with or detract from the object in question.

This is why co-ordinated ranges, such as those produced by Laura Ashley, can be so helpful. They provide the colour scheme upon which the room can be based. You might wish to use a particular curtain fabric, choosing the paint and wallpaper in complementary designs, and then picking out one or two of the main colours in the rest of the room. However, it is important to use a co-ordinated range carefully, leaving scope for adding your own personality and keeping the very element of decorating that makes it such fun – the individuality. In order to be able to do this successfully, you need to identify the key colours in the range, and then find either toning or harmonizing colours or one that provides a clear contrast. However, it is important that you make sure you do not introduce more than one colour to the scheme, or it may start to look bitty.

The principles of colour

It is the illusory nature of colour that causes so many problems to the would-be colourist or decorator, since colours are not static – our perception of them alters so that the effect differs according to the circumstances in which we see them. Colours also affect each other, so the way you combine colours can alter the way you perceive them. For example, cowslip yellow on its own will look like a simple, fresh yellow. If you put a similar area of black next to it, it will look harder, and if you put an area of red next to it, it will look warmer.

This, as you can see, makes an enormous difference to your decorating schemes. Another important consideration is light. Light changes when it strikes different surfaces. When light strikes a black surface, most of it is absorbed. When light strikes a white surface, most of it is reflected. An opaque, coloured surface absorbs some frequencies of the spectrum and reflects others.

Colour is light perceived by the retina of the human eye, and light is a series of wavelengths. In very dim conditions, what you see has no colour at all. At higher light levels, these wavelengths are bent or refracted by differing amounts within our eyes to produce what we know as the colour spectrum. The most visible manifestation of the colour spectrum is, of course, the rainbow in which the order of the colours is always the same – red, orange, yellow, green, blue and violet. In fact, violet and red are at opposite ends of the spectrum and the colours in between are simply deviations.

This monochromatic colour scheme in classic navy and gold uses bold pattern in a restrained and elegant way to create a sophisticated, yet strong, colour scheme. The beautifully dressed windows, with swagged pelmets in a navy and sand check fabric, create the focal point. The chairs are upholstered in plain cream and classic broad stripes of navy and white. Touches of bright gold, in the picture frames and tie-backs, add vitality to the decorative scheme.

13

The different types and colours of light have specific terms:

- Hue is the term used to differentiate pure colours.
- Brightness indicates the range from light to dark.
- Intensity indicates the range from a pure hue to one in which light or dark (white or black) is mixed with it.
- Tints describe the range from a pure hue to white.
- Shades indicate the range from a pure hue to black.
- Tones are the range from a pure hue to grey.
- Saturation is the term used to describe the degree of brilliance or brightness of a hue.

The psychology of colour

As well as physically perceiving colour, you also respond psychologically to colour, mostly in the same way. In other words, colours create changes of mood, which are more or less universal, in the beholder. Generally speaking, yellow lifts the spirits and induces a feeling of cheerfulness; black depresses the spirits, as can brown and purple. Red creates a strong reaction – some people find it energizing, others find it overpowering – but either way it is not a restful colour, which green is. Green soothes. Blue induces moods of reflectivity and tranquillity. White appears pure, but may not be particularly restful. The shades in between these colours will vary in their effect and impact according to how much of the other colours they contain.

In certain situations, the psychology of colour has been employed quite deliberately by professional designers, for example both in interior decorating and in packaging. Red is the colour of danger and of urgency, which is why the sign for the Red Cross is red on a white ground. Equally, red is the colour of fire and passion, which is why so many red flowers are sent around Valentine's Day.

Colours also have symbolic connotations as well as psychological significance, although the symbolism varies according to the country in question. In the West, white is the colour of purity and is therefore a traditional choice for weddings. In Latin America, purple is the colour of death. In Moslem countries, green is a holy colour. Certain colours are also perceived to be masculine or feminine. Generally, darker colours and stronger hues – such as dark greens, reds and navys – are masculine, while pastels and paler hues – such as apple greens, pinks and powder blues – are seen as feminine. However, combining the two with a novel contrasting colour – such as tobacco brown with pink or fuchsia pink with dark green – or using a masculine, geometric pattern with the pinks and a floral pattern with the dark greens, can subtly alter the usual psychological connotations.

The dramatic colours of autumn are shown here, with the scarlet leaves of the acer tree forming a vivid still life. Nature often provides inspiration for stunning colour schemes.

Generally, the most successful schemes have a limited palette of two or three principal colours, perhaps with touches here and there of other colours. If you want to vary the atmosphere, a tonal decorating scheme can be very effective – you can use several tones of one colour (adding white or black to the colour, but not changing the basic hue – in other words not adding a particular colour). This is especially successful with a very limited palette – perhaps one colour – as it breaks up the monotony and adds texture, depth and vibrancy to the whole scheme. It has been used by many successful interior designers, and is very effective for highlighting architectural detailing.

It is important, when using more than one colour, to think carefully about colour balance. How much of any one colour do you want to use, and to what extent will it dominate the other colours used? As a rule of thumb, the brighter the colour, the smaller the amount of it that you should use, as it will tend to overwhelm any duller colours that accompany it. If, for example, your scheme is mainly the colour that the Georgians called drab (this is a dirty khaki, and goes with a surprising number of other hues) matched with, for example, very small amounts of a bright cobalt blue, you will have a distinguished-looking scheme. If, on the other hand, you opted for large quantities of bright cobalt blue with touches of drab, the result would quite different. That is because it is the proportions that count when colour-mixing, not only the colours used. Quantities are therefore extremely important in this delicate matter of colour combining, and it is not an easy point to grasp until you see a successful scheme translated into its negative image. It then becomes clear why one works and the other does not.

Colour balance

Mixing colours

Companies like Laura Ashley introduce new colourways and new designs in their collections each year. Their designers have professional expertise in mixing colour and pattern, and you can use this to your advantage by choosing their pre-mixed colours and patterns. You can, if you wish, redecorate your home each time you see a new textile design that you like but, if you prefer, you can gradually mix different colours, patterns and fabrics yourself to create a more personalized look that you can add to as it suits you. The aim of this chapter is to help you to do just that, by telling you the principles that interior decorators use when mixing colour, so that you have some basis on which to plan and design a scheme yourself.

Combining several colours and patterns in a decorative scheme is certainly not new – the Victorians took it to a high art in their colour schemes known as polychromy – but it requires more discipline and a better eye than simply limiting the colour scheme to one, or perhaps two, colours. For the less sure, a limited colour scheme is definitely a valid starting point for a simplified design.

Multi-coloured effects, however, look most effective when based on an inherent plan. First, you need to decide which colours you will combine – but how do you make this initial, elementary choice? Inspiration for colours, and colour schemes, can be found in the most unexpected places. The secret is to take note of the objects that surround you – both in your own home and in the landscape – and to see which colours inspire you, or fire your imagination. There are myriad colour hues to choose from, and the differences between them can be very subtle indeed. Nature usually provides us with the best source of inspiration – from flowers and fruit to fields and landscapes – but there are man-made sources too, many of which are associated with design and decoration, from fine art and architecture, the decorative arts, furniture, ceramics, packaging and trends in the fashion world through to the printed textiles which we use in interior decoration.

Keeping a notebook in which to write down items or colours of particular interest will help, and you may find that you develop a particular taste or inclination towards a certain range of colours, or particular light or dark tones, which help to define your own taste. The colour collages (see pages 27–37) illustrate the spectrum of colours at your disposal, and have been made of up of a variety of items, both textiles and paints, and natural sources of colour and texture, to illustrate how texture and pattern can affect colour.

In days gone by, you were usually advised not to mix patterns (and, as a consequence, colours), because of the clashes you were likely to create. Pattern-mixing has become far more fashionable now, and the variety of patterns available has made it easier, but it still requires careful planning to make it work. However, there are certain basic principles

Strong primary colours – blue, red and yellow – require a bold treatment. Here, the contrast between fully saturated (i.e. colours at their brightest) blues, reds and yellows helps to ensure that the colours work well together, with no single colour dominating. The use of purple, for the cushions, helps to bridge the gap between the red and blue and bring them into harmony (purple is made from red and blue), while the large expanses of plain colour draw your attention to the textures in the room – glossy silks, sheeny walls, translucent curtains and rough sisal on the floor.

which you can follow that will help to ensure success, and they are described here.

The best method is to choose a series of colours that are balanced in some way – a similar intensity of hue, for example – and which ideally leave white out of the equation unless you are mixing neutral colours together. Used with stronger or brighter colours, white tends to be divisive, and may create the jarring, restless effect that you need to avoid when playing with several colour combinations. Nevertheless, white and shades of off-white, especially when used for ceilings, can lighten a room and make the colours appear more vivid. The use, or exclusion, of white in a decorative scheme will depend on the effect you wish to create and, probably, the amount of natural light in the room.

Good choices for a mixed colour palette include claret, forest green, classic navy and gold; speedwell blue, taupe and cream; and pale plaster pink, olive green, chambray blue and ochre. Mixing more than four colours is probably pushing your luck a little too far. Two other considerations are the quantities of colours being used and the proportions of the room. You should try to avoid using equal amounts of each colour; instead, focus attention on two colours as the major theme, and use the other colour in the supporting role as an accent colour.

As with painting, the aim is to ensure that any colour you use is not employed in isolation but is picked up as a leitmotif of the whole scheme. If you have used ochre for the walls, make sure that it reappears again in a background pattern on, say, the cushions. A dusty pink used for the frieze and ceiling could be repeated in a patterned fabric that picks out ochre, pink and one of the other colours – perhaps blue. Simple stripes of blue and pink could be used for one chair; the same fabric in an ochre and green colourway could be used for another chair, which has a similar shape.

Regency stripes have long been a popular choice for dining rooms. Here they are given a new twist in terracotta and cream rather than in the more familiar combination of vermilion and white, and are used for the blinds rather than the walls. The effect is more subtle and restrained, while still having a strong classical tradition. The colours are a wonderful foil for the oil painting over the fireplace.

Neutral colour schemes can work very well with antique furniture and classic surroundings, as this simple and restrained dining room proves. Wallpaper is often eschewed in neutrals schemes, but here it works brilliantly in a monochromatic design. The antiqued cream fireplace is the perfect complement to the fine paintings and antique furniture.

Ensuring that there is a connection of form and/or colour is one of the secrets of avoiding bittiness in such a scheme. In other words, try to repeat the shapes of, say, the soft furnishings when using mixed colours to keep some kind of continuity in the room. Alternatively, if you are using a fairly simple colour palette, you could introduce different outlines and forms of furnishing to add visual interest. Another secret which it is important to remember is the use of similar types of wood or fabric. It is best not to use several kinds of wood as well as a range of fabric types and weights. For the latter, keep to simple cottons, or perhaps luxurious silks and velvets. Mixing colours and fabric types is likely to lead to a disturbing clash of ideas. Keep the contrasts of materials for the more uniform schemes – changing the texture in a neutrals scheme, for example, is the key to bringing this type of scheme to life.

Painted surfaces give you the chance to experiment with combinations of different tones and colours: you can use stencils, rubber stamps or wooden blocks to create a wide range of patterns with subtle or distinct variations within the same hue, and without using white as a contrast. Again, picking out one colour from a multi-coloured stencil (composed perhaps of taupe, olive, blue and sand) for the paintwork (in olive) would allow you to use more than one colour, but in a discreet and unobtrusive way. You could use these particular colours in various soft pattern combinations of stripes, checks and florals, provided you keep the tonal values much the same. The scheme will not work if you use several shades of the same colour. When using three or more colours, therefore, it becomes increasingly important to keep the tonal values the same. When using one colour, you can increase the interest by using three or more tones.

Try mixing lots of pale sorbet colours together, such as apple green, sapphire blue, pale yellow and powder pink. Then add plenty of white to keep the scheme light before adding an accent colour of deep pink or turquoise. Alternatively, you could use lots of very light tones, such as pale cream, pale yellow and white, for the walls and furniture, and then add a dark accent colour such as navy blue or forest green. You could try the decorative scheme in reverse, with a dark blue room and burgundy and green upholstery, and add splashes of gold and cream highlights. You could mix solid blocks of bright colours for a jazzy effect, or mix tones of dark colours. The options are endless. Some examples of the different effects that are created by using lighter and darker tones in a decorative scheme are shown on pages 44–9. Deciding which colours to mix is a very personal matter, and everyone has their particular favourites.

Five classic colours

There are some colours which have become classics in the Laura Ashley colour palette over the past twenty years, and which appear in many of the company's paint, wallpaper and fabric designs. Five of the most popular colours are listed on these two pages, with brief descriptions of how each colour came into existence and some of the designs in which it appears. Each colour corresponds to one of the colour chapters in this book. Shown here are taupe, cowslip, moss, sapphire and rose, and each colour has been illustrated with a small colour panel to show what it looks like. You will also see these colours illustrated in the colour collages on pages 28–37.

Taupe

Taupe is one of the neutral colours in the Laura Ashley colour palette. It is a pale brown which was first introduced as a ground colour in the fruit prints such as Blueberry chintz, but which has expanded recently into a range of checks, stripes and plains to suit contemporary styling. *Taupe* is the French word for mole, and it reflects the influence of French style on the collection. When used on its own, taupe needs other neutrals and differing textures to bring it to life and create a very sophisticated look. In floral prints, taupe can be combined with pale pastels, such as in the Melrose drawing room fabric.

By the end of the 1980s, the introduction of cowslip to the Laura Ashley home furnishings collection met the need for a new decorating colour. Cowslip brings a contemporary feel to more traditional fabric designs and can be used for a clean, sunny look in older homes as well as in new ones. The Lyme Regis wallpaper in cowslip and the Alba Rose chintz were both very popular. The chintz was a striking floral bouquet spaced on a white ground, and an example of a traditional print being given a modern look by the use of colour. Cowslip yellow was also used in the Sweet Pea range of wallpapers and fabrics, and these have the enduring appeal of a country garden in the height of summer.

Cowslip

In recent years, the variety of greens in the collection has been considerably expanded. At first there were four principal greens – dark green, sage, moss and apple. Of these, moss was the shade that was used most often, both in combination with other colours and by itself. In the mono colour prints Sweet Alyssum and Wild Clematis, moss was used with white to create a wonderfully fresh look. It is a true mid-green, a clean green, neither too yellow nor too dark, and is perfect for any room that brings the outdoors into the house, such as a conservatory.

Moss

This is a very distinctive Laura Ashley colour which is hard to find in the colour palettes of other collections. It is as near as you can get to a romantic blue. Sapphire is a pale blue with a hint of lilac, and can look soft and gauzy when mixed with white. Laura Ashley herself decorated a bedroom at her house in France with a sapphire and white print, like a toile de Jouy, with white-painted furniture. Slightly deeper tones of sapphire and white can create a fresh, crisp and clean look. Sapphire works well with other colours such as rose and cowslip, and it suits a variety of climates, adding warmth to rooms in cool climates and looking bright and contemporary in hotter places.

Sapphire

Rose is a classic Laura Ashley colour – a soft blue-pink which creates a gentle and romantic room. The shade was chosen by Laura Ashley herself to suit Victorian rose prints without giving too sweet or synthetic an effect, and to sit well with other colours in the collection. For many years, rose pink was the best-selling Laura Ashley colour and was an ingredient of many beautiful textile and wallpaper collections, including simple stencil prints such as Cottage Sprig.

Rose

Mixing patterns

It is quite difficult to mix unusual colours successfully by instinct, although some people succeed without knowing why. The answer to successful mixing lies in balancing the elements of hue, tone, and tint to achieve the effect you want. In other words, it is not so much a question of whether blue goes with green, or purple goes with yellow, but the shade of blue with the shade of green, the shade of purple with the shade of yellow, and how much of each you are using in the overall scheme.

You can mix all kinds of patterns together, if you wish, provided you follow a few basic rules, which are similar to those on proportion that were outlined on page 15. If you are going to mix patterns, as a general rule you should choose ones that have similarly sized basic shapes. In other words, mix a small, sprigged floral print with a gingham, or put a big cabbage-rose pattern with wide, bold stripes. The impact will be lost if you combine a tiny Victorian flower sprig with large, dramatic stripes because the latter will dominate the former. On the other hand, a small tonal check can look wonderful with a splashy, painterly floral. Placing solid blocks of colour somewhere in a scheme of mixed colours will help to unite it and stop it looking too bitty.

Mixing certain kinds of pattern together – checks and stripes, for example – can work very well but you will probably find that it pays to keep the base colour of the fabrics the same, so that there is a consistent link between them. Mixing patterns has become a popular theme in recent years, and you can use the idea in a variety of ways, such as making cushions out of two or three different fabrics (in a simplified version of patchwork), or lining curtains, for example, with a patterned fabric rather than a plain one, or a differing colourway of the same fabric.

There is much to be said for rooms that look as though the contents have been assembled with love and care over a long period rather than decorated in one big shopping spree. The latter may look smart initially, but they also tend to feel impersonal. Some of the early twentieth-century decorators went to considerable lengths to try to create a lived-in, natural look for their clients' newly decorated houses. Nancy Lancaster, of Colefax & Fowler, used to dye new chintz in tea to remove its shiny patina and give the fabric that homely, faded, lived-in look that is the hallmark of English country house style. In recent years there has been a trend towards recycling and renovating existing furniture and fabrics. You can re-use fabrics by cutting them into borders and linings, for example, or cushions. By creating a multi-patterned look, you give yourself a great opportunity to incorporate these recycled elements – patches on an armchair or sofa taken from the previous worn covers, adding borders to pelmets or curtains, simple patchwork-style cushions or footstools covered in pieces cut from old curtains.

OPPOSITE *This is a singularly beautiful studio. Its arched double-storey window has been given a surprisingly soft and gentle treatment in pastel pinks, straw and apple greens. Mixing pattern, as here, can help to create a sense of vitality, provided the colours are kept to a limited palette. These Laura Ashley fabrics were inspired by the Omega Workshop designs of the Bloomsbury artists Vanessa Bell and Duncan Grant, which can be seen at their home, Charleston in East Sussex.*

Juxtapositions of colour

Yellow is one of the most invigorating colours in the decorator's palette, and also one of the most versatile. It is used in this Sydney sitting room in a sophisticated scheme with elegant white plasterwork which enhances the sunny, airy feel of the room. The clean lines of the ironwork chairs and the black and white chair covers and rug provide a strong visual contrast with the plain walls.

Another important element of colour mixing is the way you position the colours to achieve the greatest impact. You can play with colour harmonies (colours that complement each other) or with colour contrasts (which gain their effect from being opposite each other on the colour wheel), and to some extent you can use both together in interior decoration, provided you do so with caution.

It might help if you see your room like a painter's canvas. The bare, undecorated room is the plain, primed canvas that the painter starts with. Some painters begin with a pure white canvas, others prefer to give the canvas a dark, all-over tone. Using the first scheme, you use the natural lightness of the canvas as a starting point, and you could compare this with a room in which you have painted the walls a light shade of white or a pastel. With the toned canvas, you are starting with a predominantly darker shade, and adding lighter or darker colours to it. Whichever way you start, as with any form of painting, you block in the larger areas of colour first, and this is a perfectly sensible approach for decorating a room, too. So, choose your wall and ceiling colours, and your floor colour, first. It may be that the room has little natural light and you wish to add to it, in which case you might choose a pale colour for the walls and floor. Equally, you may wish to turn the lack of natural light into a decorating virtue, in which case you will keep the scheme deliberately dark and dramatic. Either way, the walls and floors will provide you with the backdrop. Having decided on these two elements, it is time to think about

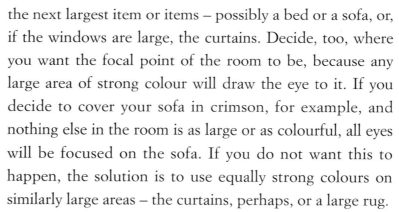

the next largest item or items – possibly a bed or a sofa, or, if the windows are large, the curtains. Decide, too, where you want the focal point of the room to be, because any large area of strong colour will draw the eye to it. If you decide to cover your sofa in crimson, for example, and nothing else in the room is as large or as colourful, all eyes will be focused on the sofa. If you do not want this to happen, the solution is to use equally strong colours on similarly large areas – the curtains, perhaps, or a large rug.

As soon as you add pattern to the colour, you change the way it is perceived from a distance. A red and white pattern, for example, when seen from a distance will no longer appear predominantly red but will look pinkish instead. By adding other touches of red, such as red cushions to a red and white checked chair, you concentrate attention on the redness of the red and white

pattern. Adding white cushions will make the pattern appear to be paler and lighter.

Colour contrasts can also be used to weaken or strengthen colours – two similarly strong, contrasting colours will more or less cancel each other out. If you use four strong colours, they will each have less impact than if you used just one of these plus white, for example, or a less saturated toning colour.

Just as colour contrasts play an important part in decorating decisions, so too does tone. Darker or lighter shades of the same colour hue can create a very different impression, and you can use tones in a variety of ways to add interest to the scheme, from simply changing the tone of a single colour on the walls (see pages 100–1), to shifting the focus in the room by using lighter colours at one end and darker tones at the other, rather like the negative and positive images of a photograph.

You cannot play with colour without considering shape, because colour and light will draw attention to form. As the Neutrals and Naturals chapter explains, when colour is absent, shape and texture become the main focus of interest, but another way of drawing attention to shape is to use a single bright colour in a neutral surround. One very bright item in a monochrome scheme will obviously draw attention to that item, and your eye will be drawn to both its colour and its form, so this presents you with another means of creating certain key elements in a decorative scheme. An electric-blue vase sitting in a white alcove on a wall, with no other bright colours nearby, will draw the eye, so that the object becomes a major focus of interest. If this item is plain, rather than patterned, the eye will be drawn to its outline against the contrasting background. If it is patterned – such as a Chinese porcelain vase – the pattern itself will become the focus.

There are various small ways in which you can use colour to draw attention to shape and form. Piping cushions on a sofa or chair will have the effect of defining the outline and the overall shape of the piece of furniture, and the greater the contrast between the base fabric and the piping, the more obvious this becomes. Small touches like this are a decorator's tricks to channel and focus the eye on the places where you wish it to rest. When they are subtle, they are almost imperceptible, but nevertheless they play a part in the overall success of the scheme and should not be ignored.

A Lloyd Loom chair in eau-de-Nil makes a strong statement of shape against the brilliant blue clapboard walls of a loggia. Although these colours would not, in all probability, have been planned together, they show that simple shapes and clean colours combine to make an extremely effective decorative statement.

If you are unsure of your abilities in terms of mixing colours, then try to keep the scheme as simple as possible and gradually introduce more detail and pattern when you are sure that the basis is correct. Never add the detail in one area alone. It must be done with a sense of balance – an ability to consider the whole effect.

Practical decorating with colour

If you are planning a decorative scheme for any room, it will help you enormously if you take a tip from the professionals and make what they call a storyboard. To all extents and purposes, this is rather like a child's scrapbook. You simply collate the various coloured elements in the room – either using actual samples, or blobs of paint or coloured pens – on a single sheet of paper. It helps if you try to keep the coloured elements in ratio to each other – for example, you could make the coloured blob for the walls six times the size of the fabric swatch representing the sofa. Represent every coloured element, including the trimming and piping, and do not forget the floor covering. For example, even if it is simply a stripped wooden floor you should represent it on the storyboard with a suitably sized blob of similarly coloured paint. By putting these elements together, and making any informative notes at the same time, you will find it far easier to plan and pull the scheme together than if you were trying to keep all the ideas in your head.

You will probably find it simplest to compile the storyboard on a large piece of A3, or even Imperial size paper, to fit in all the elements in proportion to one another. You can attach pieces of paper bearing the coloured paint blobs to save having to redo the storyboard if you change your mind half-way through the scheme.

Compiling a storyboard becomes much easier if you have a good collection of reference material. Keep any magazine articles showing decorative schemes that particularly appeal to you, and have at hand the paint cards produced by manufacturers of good-quality paint who specialize in interesting colour ranges.

The colour charts

To give you an idea of the different hues and tints of the principal colours discussed in this book, five colour charts have been created from a range of fabrics, papers, paints and natural materials, and include some Laura Ashley designs and colourways. These charts are intended to give a taste of the vast range of shades that are available in each particular colour and the variety of possibilities that can be drawn on for inspiration.

As a general rule, the purest colour is located in the centre of the chart, with the lighter tints above and the darker tones below. If you read across the chart, from left to right, you will see how a colour changes, according to what has been mixed with it. In the blue chart, you will find greener blues (those with yellow added to pure blue) on the left, and more mauve blues (those with more red added to the pure blue) on the right. As a result, you can begin to see the subtle differences in hue, tint and saturation which are contained within a single colour theme. Colours appear at their brightest when they are seen at their purest. The pure colour is mixed with black for darker shades and with white for paler tints. Each of the charts on the following pages includes different textural elements which illustrate the ways texture can vary the colour impact of a hue – from the glossy sheen of a leaf and the silky quality of rose petals, to the natural speckles of oatmeal and the tactile, rough quality of bark.

In the colour charts on the following pages, an asterisk indicates a Laura Ashley colour.

The most elementary neutral, white, lies in the centre of this chart. To the left, the colours become cooler, with silvery greys on the far left, next to greenish-neutrals such as ash and bronze. On the right are warmer hues like cream and sand. At the bottom, the darker neutrals range from chocolate brown and rust to charcoal.

Neutrals and naturals

The chart for yellow shows how this colour can range from sharp citrus yellows with a high green content on the right, through bright, sunny, primary hues in the centre, and the more orangey-yellows, with a red content, such as saffron, yellow ochre, turmeric and orange, on the left.

Yellows

Green is made up of two primary colours, blue and yellow, and the central green in this colour chart has a more or less equal balance of these two colours. On the right of the chart are greens with more blue, such as jade and viridian. On the left are those with a strong yellow content, including olive, moss and apple. Some of the darker greens, like forest and Paris green, are tinted with black to give them a deeper, darker tone.

Greens

In this chart, you can easily see the movement of colour from green shades of blue, such as kingfisher and smoke, which are on the left, to red shades of blue, such as sapphire and delphinium, on the right.

Blues

Poppy and scarlet are the primary colours in this chart and sit in the centre. To the right are the shades of brick, fresco, terracotta and russet, which contain yellow, ochre or white. To the left are pinker reds, such as raspberry and deep pink, which are bluer and more purple in nature than the primary hues. The top row shows the softer, pale tones of rose pink, with a high white content, such as crushed strawberry and plaster pink, which contrast with the more vivid pinks below.

Reds

Black and white

Dove grey

Oatmeal

*Ivory

White

Warm grey

Silver

Ash

Pumice

Pale taupe

Slate

Earl Grey

Wainscot

Raw linen

*Taupe

Peat

Charcoal

Bronze

Chocolate

Nut brown

Calico

*Stone

String

Oyster

Aran

*Natural

Silver birch

Biscuit

*Cream

*Sand

Desert

Mushroom

Rust

Jute

Nutmeg

Fawn

Mocha

Coffee

Clay

Bark

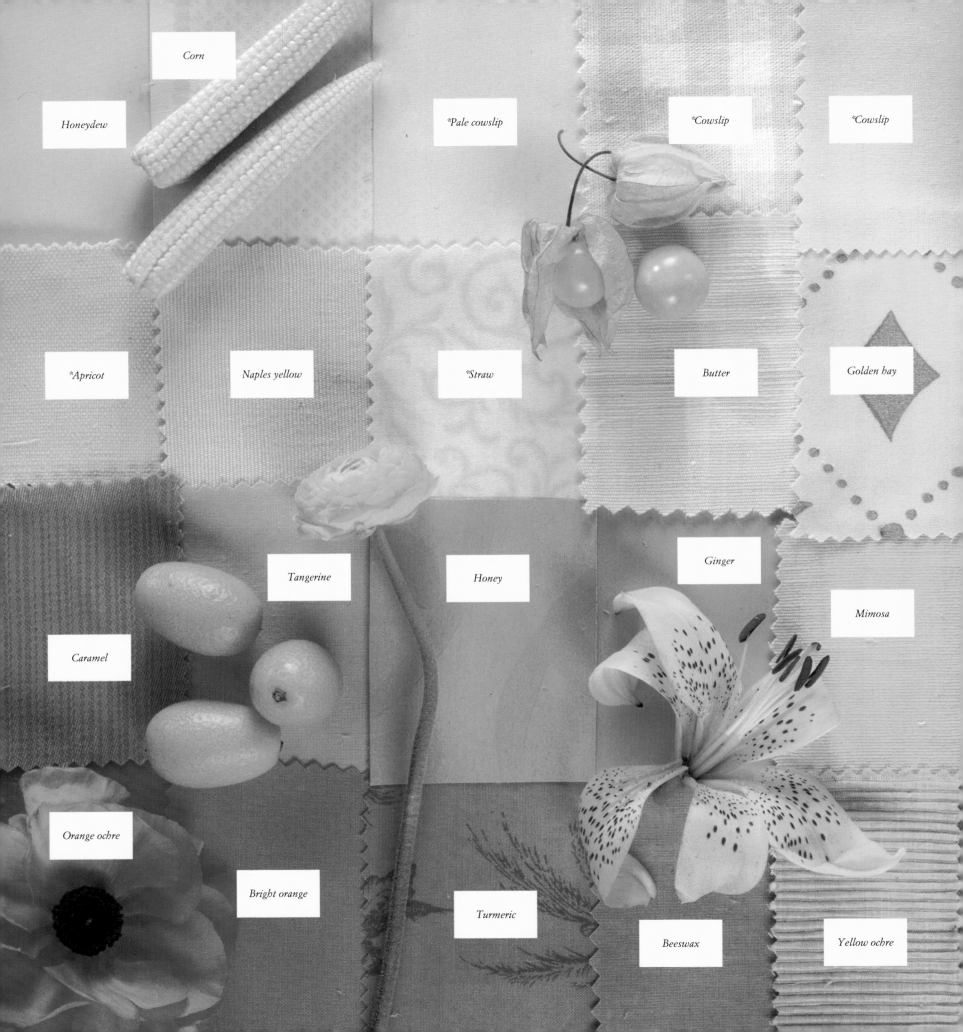

Honeydew

Corn

*Pale cowslip

*Cowslip

*Cowslip

*Apricot

Naples yellow

*Straw

Butter

Golden hay

Tangerine

Honey

Ginger

Caramel

Mimosa

Orange ochre

Bright orange

Turmeric

Beeswax

Yellow ochre

Butter

Primrose

Citrus yellow

Powder yellow

Pale gold

Buttercup

Lemon

*Old gold

Camomile

Savannah

Primary yellow

*Deep cowslip

Old gold

Pale mustard

Orchard yellow

Mustard

Golden rod

Eastern gold

Saffron

Paprika

Olive

*Pale moss

Lichen

Mint

Apple

Khaki

Grass green

Sage

Emerald

*Moss

Deep olive

Hedgerow green

*Dark moss

Rainforest

Deep emerald green

Spruce

Autumn green

*Aragon green

*Dark green

Malachite

*Pale heath green

Pistachio

Seaspray

Pale jade

Aquamarine

*Heath green

*Fir green

*Jade

*Jade

Turquoise

Rosemary

*Ely green

Bottle green

*Viridian

Deep viridian

Nettle

Racing green

*Paris green

Forest

Hunting green

Pale Adam blue

Duck egg

Cloud

Powder blue

Porcelain blue

Wedgwood blue

Adam blue

Azure

Sky blue

Dusty blue

Cerulean blue

*Smoke

Deep powder blue

Warm smoke

*China blue

Atlantic blue

Kingfisher

*Prussian

Peacock

*Midnight

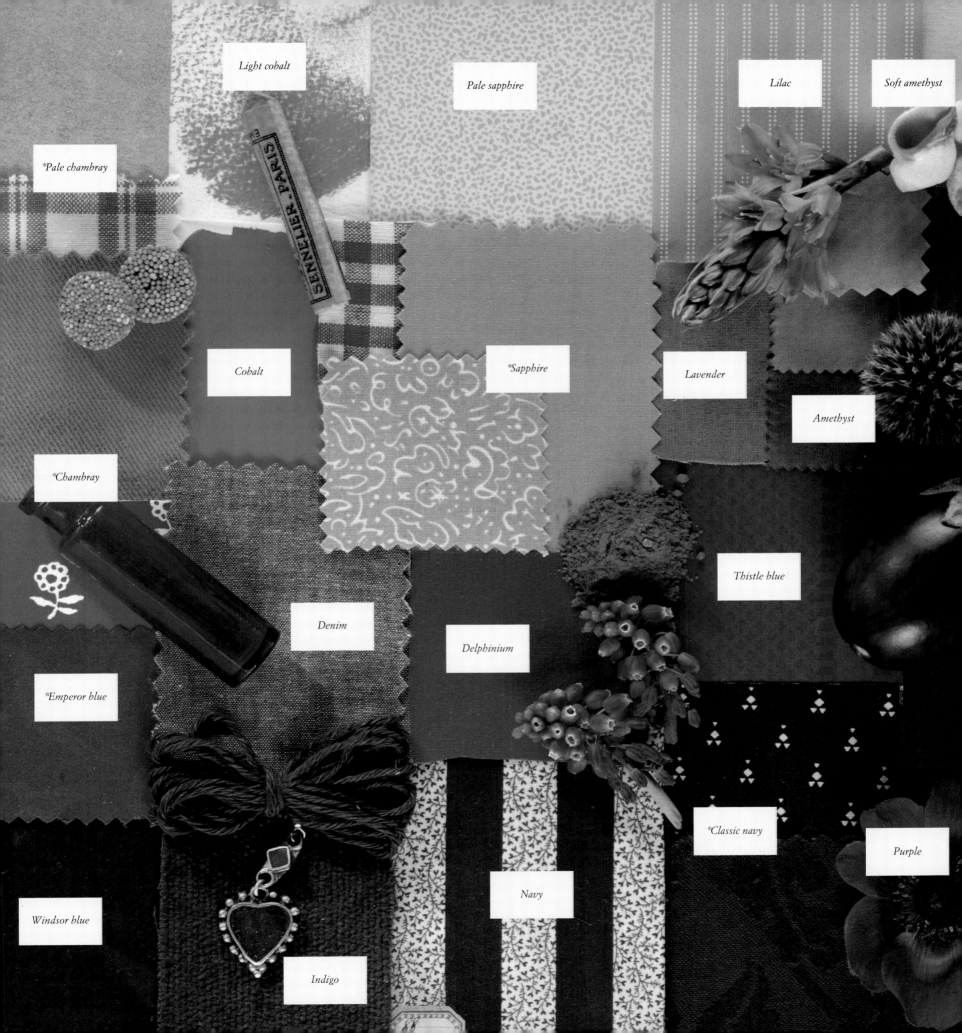

*Pale chambray

Light cobalt

Pale sapphire

Lilac

Soft amethyst

Cobalt

*Sapphire

Lavender

Amethyst

*Chambray

Thistle blue

*Emperor blue

Denim

Delphinium

*Classic navy

Purple

Windsor blue

Navy

Indigo

Pale plum

Shell pink

*Rose

Powder pink

*Old rose

*Plum

Deep rose

Rose pink

*Crushed strawberry

Dusty pink

Mulberry

Raspberry

Magenta

*Crimson

Primary red

Morello

Scarlet

Ruby

Claret

*Burgundy

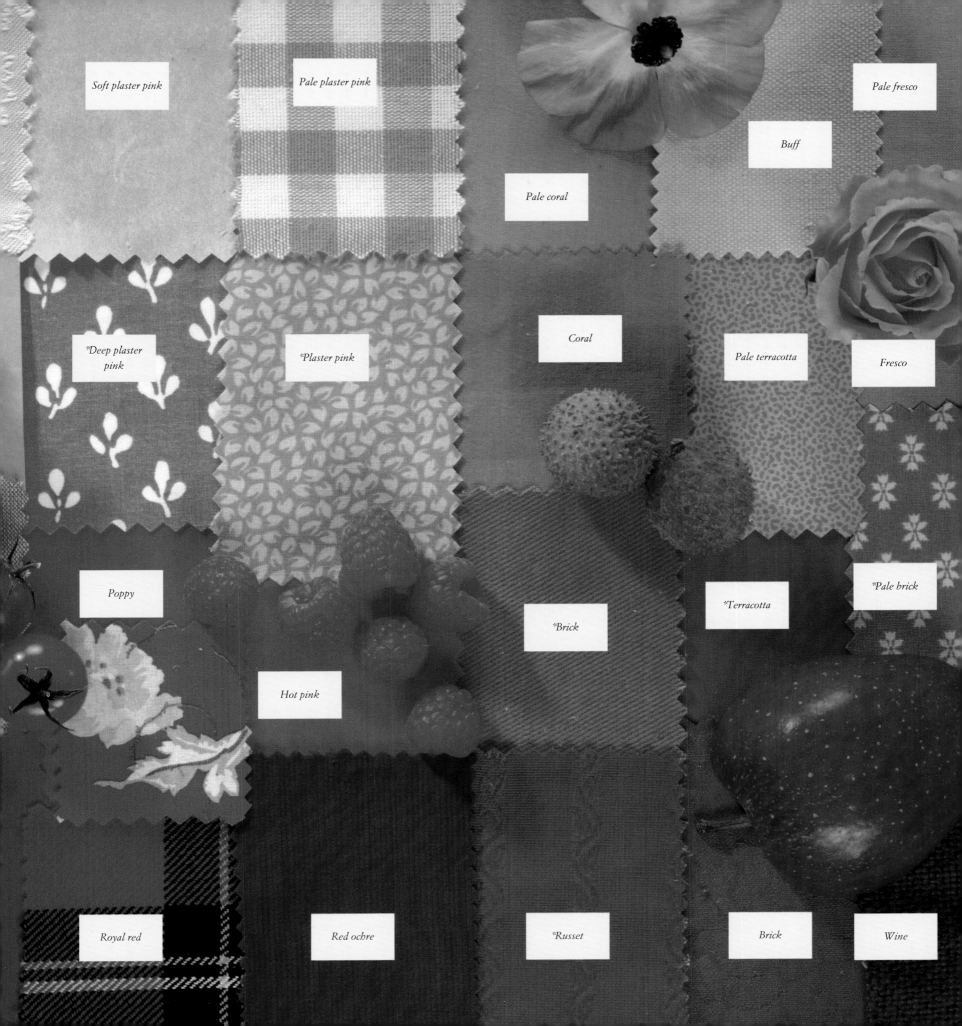

Soft plaster pink

Pale plaster pink

Pale fresco

Buff

Pale coral

*Deep plaster pink

*Plaster pink

Coral

Pale terracotta

Fresco

Poppy

*Pale brick

*Terracotta

*Brick

Hot pink

Royal red

Red ochre

*Russet

Brick

Wine

Period colours

You may decide that you wish to decorate your house or flat in colours that were typical of the period in which it was built. Although various august institutions who care for historic houses have done a great deal of research into historical colours, you may find it more practical or harmonious to use colours that are approximate, and suggest the period, rather than those that are absolutely correct. This is true of pattern as well as colour. Many of the modern fabric designs are reworkings of designs stored in the world's museums and archives. Sometimes the new design has an updated colour theme, colours which have been made less garish and more dusty to represent colour before the use of chemical dyes, or a slightly revised pattern. In cases like these, it is the colour that will determine whether the fabric is appropriate rather than how close the pattern is to the original. You can read some excellently researched books on the history of interiors, many copiously illustrated with plates of coloured drawings that were often produced by the decorator of the period.

How closely you wish to follow any original colour scheme or style depends on the architecture of your home as much as anything else. Unfortunately, many houses have been modernized at the expense of the architect's original plans for the building, with period features being lost or replaced by contemporary equivalents. Certain colours predominated in various eras, usually influenced by the materials available, and often by particular trendsetters of the time. All colour used in decoration before the Industrial Revolution in the nineteenth century relied on naturally occurring pigments, and the colours popular in different countries were influenced by what was available locally. The names given to the colours, which are still used today, tend to reflect the place of origin of the pigment. For example, burnt sienna, which is a rich, reddish-brown, comes from Siena in Italy, and raw umber, which is a more greyish-brown, comes from Umbria, also in Italy. Those local pigments are likely to influence local colour schemes, so you often see houses painted in deep, rich reds where the local earth pigment is red oxide, or in deep yellows where the local pigment is yellow ochre.

Some of the pigments are common to many parts of the world, whereas others are rare and therefore precious. Such colours were often too expensive for domestic use, and eventually cheaper substitutes were found. The rich, deep colours of the Renaissance period – the golds, lapis lazuli, cobalt blues, ruby reds, deep greens and porphyry greens – relied on some of the more expensive pigments. Heavy hangings, velvets and weighty furniture characterized the style, as any glance around a gallery of Renaissance paintings will show. With the turn of the seventeenth century, the style and colour palette lightened and changed. Baroque and rococo, with their emphasis on swirling movement and light

OPPOSITE Walls painted in toning blue and bluish-green give a wonderful feeling of translucency and depth. Texture becomes extremely important when you use subtle, simple colour combinations, and the figured silk of the elegant sofa and chairs, and the thick pile of the carpet, are thrown into relief in this eighteenth-century room at Mount Vernon, Virginia. It is the family home of George Washington, and has been furnished and decorated exactly as it would have been when Washington was alive.

The yellow and white Staircase Hall at Hatchlands in Surrey is a classic example of the early work of the architect, Robert Adam. If you wish to display any kind of sculpture, you need a setting which allows attention to focus on its form. Neutrals schemes – here, yellow, white, black and brown – are ideal for this purpose since they recede, allowing the artefacts to take pride of place. Note how the light catches the texture of the statues, making a wonderful play of shadow and enhancing the form.

colours, introduced a whole new era in the colour palette for the interior, with the use of pastel shades of pink, blue, pale green, gold and white.

By the mid-eighteenth century, the colour palette, although still light, became more prolific, thanks to the work of Robert Adam, the renowned Scottish architect. Adam, having taken the Grand Tour in the 1750s, brought back the sunshine colours from Italy, and his colour schemes, richly adorned with stucco work, were in mid-tones of green, blue and violet, with white, and sometimes gold, as relief. With the revival of Classicism, this lightheartedness went and a more drab and formal decorating style intervened. The emphasis of the Palladian revival was on form rather than on ornamentation, and a duller colour palette ensured that the classical lines were emphasized. Drab – a particularly dull greeny-brown – was one of the colours, often offset with putty colour, white or pale grey.

Fabrics

The range of fabrics at your disposal is so extensive that you can feel spoilt for choice. However, there are a few rules worth noting. If possible, start with a relatively clear idea of what you are looking for – the colour, type of pattern or atmosphere of your finished room may be enough to set you on the right track. Try not to spend too long gazing at pattern samples at any one time, otherwise your eye may become confused. If possible, choose times for browsing around shops when they are not full of busy shoppers who may jostle or distract you, are not about to close for the night, and when the staff will be available to give you their attention and advice.

Try to ensure that you have a clear idea of the weight and texture of the fabric that you need, such as an upholstery weight for soft furnishings. Having chosen the fabric, keep a swatch in your notebook so that you can refer to it when choosing other decorative elements such as braids, piping or cushions. Colour-matching different fabrics and trimmings by memory alone is at best hit and miss and, at worst, disastrous and a waste of money.

Fabric weights and finishes come in a vast range these days, but you need to choose one that is suitable for the purpose you have in mind. Today, most fabrics are graded, as they are in the Laura Ashley range, by function – for drape; for drape and upholstery; for upholstery; for sheers; and for linings. You can, of course, ignore these gradings, but if so you will have to be careful because there are always sound reasons why the fabrics have been so categorized. You can use lining fabrics as top fabrics, if you wish, or use top fabrics as linings, provided they are roughly the same weight. Mattress ticking, now frequently used as a top fabric, was once deemed suitable only as a functional fabric. You can also create your own fabrics by stitching and piecing them together to make borders, stripes and even patchworks of pattern and colour.

Sage green, yellow ochre and Indian red are all tints of purer colours to which black has been added, so that they appear less demanding and more subtle. Because they have roughly the same tonal values, they tend to cancel each other out, creating a scheme that is more neutral in feel than a description of the colours involved would lead you to suspect.

Paint There is an increasingly good range of paints on the market, many of them manufactured by specialists in their field. Although they cost slightly more than most paints, they have the advantage of a more subtle range of colours and a limited colour palette. This may sound like a contradiction in terms, but just as too many fabrics can confuse your eye for pattern and colour, so extensive paint charts can create a form of blindness – you may feel unable to make a choice and in a panic you could opt for something unsuitable or disappointing.

With paint, it is not only the question of choosing the right shade – you need also to find an appropriate paint for the task in hand. There are various paint compositions available, which are determined by the ingredients used. Originally, paint was basically pigment and chalk turned into a paste-like solution, with water or oil as the binding agent. With the mechanization of the paint industry during the Industrial Revolution and subsequent advances in the chemical industry, paints have become increasingly sophisticated and varied. You are now offered an almost infinite range of types of paint – including vinyl emulsions, gloss paints, floor paints and outdoor paints, all in a variety of finishes – and a whole new range of paint-like substances, in the form of woodstains, have recently come on the market. You therefore have to consider what you want to paint, and the best medium to use for the job in hand. Paints

Adam green was one of the most popular decorating colours in the eighteenth century. It lends itself marvellously to displays of wooden furniture and paintings, which perhaps explains why it has long been popular as a decorating colour for large country houses. Here, at Homewood House in Baltimore, the colour has been deepened to varying shades of apple green, while keeping the overall Adam style. White plasterwork, another classic Adam feature, helps to define and focus attention on the architecture.

available from good-quality manufacturers, and particularly from traditional paint manufacturers, are increasingly including old-fashioned finishes, such as distemper and flat oil paint. Originally, distemper contained lime to help prevent mould spores forming – a necessity in houses with no damp course, and one of the reasons why sculleries and larders were often distempered. Unlike modern vinyl paint, distemper allows the natural stone, brick or plaster it covers to breathe, allowing moisture through. Modern vinyl paint, when applied to a damp surface, will bubble and crack.

Paint, until recently, was largely only applied to walls, ceilings, doors and window frames, as well as kitchen cupboards. As the pine furniture that proliferated in many homes across several continents needed a facelift, so painted furniture has become increasingly popular. Paint finishes of various sorts have given most amateur interior decorators a chance to revitalize their homes in imaginative and original ways without spending a fortune, so it is hardly surprising that these paint effects have become a major decorating story in the 1980s and 1990s.

Wood, as opposed to plaster, can be painted in a variety of finishes, depending on whether you want the natural appearance of the wood to show through, or whether you wish to disguise it. Durability of finish is also a key point, and it often pays to varnish any paint effect, whether for furniture or for walls, to make it last longer.

Wallpaper

As with paints and fabrics, there are different types and weights of wallpaper available, designed for different purposes. Laura Ashley produces three different kinds – embossed papers, which have a relief pattern and plain finish, which you can paint to suit your colour scheme; standard wallpapers, which are plain or printed; and vinyl and matt vinyl papers, which have been coated to make them fully spongeable, and are therefore suitable for any rooms where steam may affect the paper. Borders and friezes are also available, in varying widths, which can be used by themselves or with other wallpapers.

Before wallpaper came into general use with the arrival of the Industrial Revolution which mechanized the production process, wallpaper was hand-printed, using wooden blocks, and supplied in squares or small strips. The amount of time involved in their manufacture meant they were only available to the very rich. Some manufacturing houses still supply hand-blocked papers today, but at a price. There is nothing quite like the beauty and quality of a good hand-blocked paper, but unfortunately it is very expensive. However, many companies, including Laura Ashley, can print wallpaper designs so that they resemble hand-blocked designs.

Mixing colours successfully

Although it is relatively easy to devise an interior decoration scheme using a very limited colour palette, mixing several colours together can present problems for the inexperienced home decorator because the scheme can lack unity and cohesion. The secret of successfully mixing several colours lies in choosing some large areas of plain colour, and clever mixing of tones of the same hue. In fact, the choice of tone of each colour – whether light or dark – has a very important part to play in the overall mood and atmosphere of the room.

In this deliberately constructed room set, the starting point is a palette of four 'bright' colours representing more or less similar mid-tones – pink, yellow, turquoise blue and apple green. If you do not understand what 'tone' means, screw up your eyes when you look at the photographs. Certain colours will appear lighter than others – this is what is meant by tone. It is easy to confuse tone with brightness of colour, but colours that appear bright are not always light. It is much easier to learn about the differences between tone and brightness when looking at plain colours. As soon as other colours are included, your eye is distracted and you fail to notice whether the effect is predominantly light or dark. White added to a pattern will automatically jump out at you, and may cause you to think that the overall effect is lighter than it really is, but if you half-close your eyes when you look at it again, the true tonal value of the scheme will emerge.

The colours in this room were chosen from swatches of fabric set against an expanse of yellow paper to represent the wall colour. It is crucial to begin your scheme by trying different swatches of fabric next to one another to see how they work. At the swatch stage, it is important to look at print as well as colour. In this room, a floral linen has been chosen for the curtains. The sand-coloured background is important because it is a mid-tone and therefore works with both the pale and dark schemes of this room which are shown on the following pages. The pink and turquoise upholstery colours pick out the pink and turquoise flower colours in the print. A turquoise linen border has been sewn round the edge of the curtains to give them definition against the yellow wall.

Understanding the difference between tone and brightness of colour is important because it affects the way the colours 'read' from a distance: dark colours recede and light colours advance. To make matters more difficult for you, reds look as if they are nearer than they really are and blues look further away. Balancing these factors of light and dark, and advancing and receding colours, is an important step in learning to manipulate them to achieve the effects you want, and in creating a look that is warm or cool. Colours with red and yellow in them are perceived as warm; colours containing blue and green are perceived as cool.

Here, the four principal colours have been used for the major items in the room, using the mid-tones of pink, turquoise blue and apple green for the sofas and chair, and yellow for the walls. Because the tonal values of each of these items are fairly similar, the colours balance. A shocking pink sofa, with bottle green and royal blue armchairs, would have concentrated attention on the pink sofa to the exclusion of the other two colours. You can therefore use colour choices to manipulate the effect you are trying to achieve.

In this photograph, curtains have been added to the basic room to unify the scheme. The sand-coloured linen curtains with their turquoise and pink floral pattern complement the mid-tone background and the turquoise and pink sofas.

Touches of lighter tones have now been added to the basic scheme in the form of smaller accessories, such as cushions in pale tones of the three main colours (pale pink, pale mint green and pale sky blue), throws and pale painted furniture. The overall effect is much more open and increases the feeling of space in the room. You can use this to great effect to make a small or cramped room appear larger than it is. A much paler tone on the walls would further increase the appearance of space.

In the same basic room, light accessories have been replaced with a variety of dark ones: predominantly, a selection of plain, dark cushions in deep bottle green, navy blue, deep maroon, plum and rich, raspberry red; a dark burgundy carpet; various throws on the sofa; a dark-toned large oil painting on the wall; and dark wood furniture. The effect is to deepen and enclose the space, pulling the sofas and chairs apparently closer together, and giving the room a much greater solidity.

The way we perceive colour depends in part on where and how it is positioned, and the colours which are put next to it. In these two photographs, differently toned cushions have been added to the green armchair, to show how they affect its base colour. Here, the base fabric looks darker, because the light cushions make the plain green fabric of the sofa deepen and recede.

In this photograph, two deeper-toned cushions in denim and forest green have been added to the green armchair. They lighten the colour of the fabric, and make it appear to come forward.

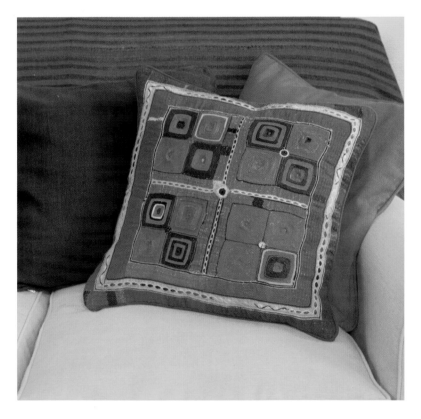

On this page, the pink sofa has been given three treatments. ABOVE LEFT *It has been given pale-toned cushions in pink and white gingham, cowslip and mint. The white in the gingham appears to come towards you.* ABOVE RIGHT *The sofa with dark-toned cushions in deep bottle green and dark maroon. They enrich and deepen the pink fabric of the sofa.* LEFT *A striped throw and a mixture of light and dark cushions have been added. The yellow on the front of the embroidered cushion makes it appear to advance towards you.*

OPPOSITE *The same exercise has been carried out on the turquoise sofa, but pattern has also been introduced.* TOP LEFT *Cushions in pale pink, eau-de-Nil and a large check have been added.* TOP RIGHT *The throw intensifies the colours in the cushions and creates a feeling of harmony.* BOTTOM LEFT *The effect in these photographs of the turquoise sofa is more muted as the contrast between light and dark decreases.* BOTTOM RIGHT *The pattern of the throw links the extremes of light and dark tones, and creates a more harmonious overall effect.*

CHAPTER 2

*neutrals
and
naturals*

The overall effect of using neutrals in decorating is to create a feeling of space, tranquillity and harmony. If you do not want an interior that might date quickly, then a neutrals scheme is almost always the sensible option. This is in part because it has been popular at so many points in the history of architecture and interior decoration – most memorably, perhaps, in the stucco and plasterwork of the Adam brothers in the eighteenth century – and in part because it enhances any architectural details, so it never truly goes out of vogue.

Although white is not strictly a colour, it is one of the most important elements in any decorative scheme, providing either the entire basis for it, or areas of contrast in any number of different colour combinations. A very large portion of the range of neutrals lies in the white, cream and beige sector, while ivories, taupes, sands, stones, jutes, browns and greys are considered to be natural colours, because they are found in natural objects and settings.

Remember when using white that it has many shades. It is not the simple, flat colour you first imagine, and the composition of the fabric, paint, plaster, paper or wood will determine the way that it reflects light, and whether as a consequence it looks warm or cold. You can play with different tones of white, making subtle shading distinctions, to create the kind of shadow that you would automatically obtain from architectural relief. This is a particularly valuable technique when you need to create some definition and interest which would not otherwise exist on a wall, perhaps because it has no architectural features or interest of its own.

Little Moreton Hall in Cheshire is considered to be the most perfect example of a timber-framed manor house anywhere in the United Kingdom. The black timbers and white-painted panels form a striking contrast and prove that a neutrals scheme can be equally as dramatic as one which uses bold colours.

It is no accident that picture or sculpture galleries are often designed with white walls and pale floors. These provide the perfect foil to show off decorative elements, be they furniture, fabrics, paintings or even people. Neutrals have been a major feature in many specific decorating styles: in the pale ice-cream colours of the stucco of Nash terraces; in the cool and spacious interiors inspired by Minimalism with its bleached floors and furniture, and white-painted walls; in the bluish-white-painted surfaces of Scandinavian style; or the simple, white-painted stone houses of the Mediterranean countries, where the reflectivity of white helps to reduce the heat by deflecting it.

Neutrals schemes rely much more on clever use of light and texture than any other colour scheme. Pale colours, whites and creams are highly reflective, so they bounce natural light off the walls and back into the room to create an airy atmosphere. The textures in the room are also enhanced because the lack of colour automatically makes you focus on the surface of objects. A combination of the two elements is the hallmark of any neutrals scheme, be it the simple, flat expanses of white-painted stone, cool marble floors and the white cotton dustsheets of an Italianate interior, or the jutes and hemps, linens, canvases and pale, bleached wood of more modern interiors. You could, very successfully, decorate a whole house with neutrals, from pale dove grey through to ochre, varying them slightly in each room, to give a subtle but wonderfully rich and textural effect that links the rooms in a harmonious theme. Whatever the look you choose, it is important to ensure it stays in character.

Light plays an essential part in any neutrals scheme, whether natural light from large windows or deliberately angled artificial lighting, since it is the play of shadows on these monochromatic surfaces that creates the real interest and atmosphere of each room. Any room in the house, from bathroom to kitchen, can be decorated with neutrals and naturals, but it is important to use the room's existing features as the cornerstone of the scheme. A cottage drawing room with dark oak beams, for example, would require a very different treatment from a barn conversion with stripped pine or elm floors. In the former, natural, soft, thick fabrics like jacquards, chenilles, crewelwork and damasks could be good choices, while in the latter you might opt for harder textures such as canvases, sailcloths and cotton reps, which are more in keeping with the sharper, cleaner lines of the architecture. The artefacts – whether roughly-hewn stone jars, simple Wedgwood creamware or delicate handblown glass – will also help to set the theme and tone, and should be selected for their ability to harmonize with both the setting and the other furnishing elements. Ensuring this continuity of texture, tone and form is the key to successful decorating in neutrals and naturals.

The influence of neutrals

Neutrals have long been used in decorative schemes, and they featured heavily in the designs of the Georgians, such as Robert Adam and John Nash, as well as later artists such as those in the Arts and Crafts movement which was particularly influential in its use of natural colours and unpolished wood. Simple domestic interiors of the past also frequently used a lot of white because it was inexpensive, bright and easy to keep clean.

The ornate, richly coloured and heavy decorative schemes of the Victorians and Edwardians, and the vivid colour schemes of the Roaring Twenties, were met by an inevitable backlash in the 1930s, when neutrals became the height of fashion. This was also the heyday of the interior decorator. Prior to this, architects, cabinet-makers, curtain-makers and upholsterers had provided the only real guidance on interior design, in a rather piecemeal fashion. After the First World War, however, the new-found emancipation of women led them to look for suitable work, and many well-to-do women found their niche in advising on the arrangement of interiors.

Although now chiefly recognized as an architect and designer of furniture, it was as an interior designer that Charles Rennie Mackintosh was best known in his lifetime (1868–1928). He employed contrasts of light and dark, in monochromatic schemes, to create an almost Japanese-like simplicity in his designs, with their consequent emphasis on form and structure. In the drawing room at Mackintosh's own house at 120 Mains Street, in his native Glasgow, he created dramatic and stark effects with just this emphasis, using white for the walls, floors and most of the furniture. The only soft element in the room came from the see-through muslin drapes over the windows – a style that has found favour again today nearly one hundred years later.

Mackintosh was the exponent, par excellence, of monochromatic effects in decoration, and it is largely thanks to his original influence that a range of black and white inspired schemes became the vogue in the Jazz Age of the 1930s. Black and white is still a popular decorative emblem today, particularly for hallways and kitchens, and sometimes conservatories, because it is an excellent way to show off decorative motifs or geometric patterns. Black and white tiled floors have long been popular in grand entrances, and black and white tiling was frequently used in newly constructed 1930s bathrooms, with plain white bathroom fittings. Today, the effect is often softened by the addition of natural wood surfaces, replacing the chrome and glass popular in the 1930s, to create a warmer, more sympathetic, but still elegant finish.

The decorative style of Syrie Maugham (1879–1955) was a natural extension of some of the principles that underpinned Charles Rennie Mackintosh's interiors. The former wife of Henry Wellcome, head of the pharmaceutical firm, and latterly married to the novelist Somerset Maugham, she became a decorator, having worked in the antiques department of the prestigious London shop, Fortnum and Mason. Her hallmark as a decorator was her penchant for light-coloured fabrics, and for stripping furniture of its previous dark stains, then either painting or waxing it to restore its original, natural, pale wood lustre – described at the time as 'pickling'.

The all-white interior which Syrie Maugham created in her London house in 1927 took this neutrals theme a stage further, but departed from the spare, sculptural lines of Charles Rennie Mackintosh. She blended ornate French Louis XIV furniture, which she stripped and waxed, or painted in pale colours, with the then popular Modernist chrome and glass, setting off the tough, uncompromising lines of modern furniture with generous swathes of plain but textured neutral fabrics. This created an eclectic mix that neatly summed up this period of massive social upheaval which followed the end of the First World War, as the old order gave way to a more classless, more mobile society.

The use of tones of cream, beige and white has recently found favour again in interior decoration, and has become a popular idiom in 1990s style. This is in part because they provide a necessary contrast with the bold colours and patterns popular in the 1980s, partly because there is growing interest in the 1990s in conservation, restoration and a more natural way of life, and also because of the growing popularity of the bleached Scandinavian look and of colours faded by the sun.

The sharper monochromatic schemes of the 1930s, with their distinct contrasts of black and white, have given way recently to much more subtle decorative schemes of grey, white and taupe, where the interplay of light and shadow lends an almost architectural feel to the overall colour scheme. Soft textures and non-reflective surfaces are very much a part of this kind of look.

Monochromatic colour schemes, in this case in black, grey and white, can be extremely effective, as the Great Hall at Syon House, Surrey, designed by Robert Adam in the 1760s, demonstrates. Spare, elegant and cool, monochromatic schemes are ideal for large, light rooms.

Style

Although predominantly white, this room benefits enormously from the touches of ochre in the warm colour of the wooden boards, the large print on the wall and pieces of occasional furniture. Without any strong colour to distract the eye, the focus is drawn to the shape of the furniture – a nicely balanced mix of hard and soft lines.

As soon as you eschew bold colour, you force the eye to concentrate on the two other key aspects of interior design: shape and texture. If you are opting for a neutrals-inspired scheme, then you are, perforce, going to draw attention to these factors, and it becomes an essential part of the style to make the most of them, whether in the form of furniture, textiles or architecture.

A neutrals scheme will draw attention to the shape of both the architecture and furniture, since the eye is not distracted by colour. If you have particularly good furniture, or a handsomely proportioned room, for example, a neutrals scheme may well be the best option. You can create the odd splash of colour in a predominantly neutrals room, which will help to bring it to life and give it focus. Clever positioning of the furniture becomes particularly important and, in this kind of scheme, the best solution can be to opt for less rather than more, keeping the attention on a few attractive pieces. This is a look that is strictly for those who like clean lines and spacious rooms.

However, there are many other neutrals schemes to choose from. You can create a minimal look with white walls, pale woods and white fabrics, or you can opt for an

eclectic and cluttered look, with pale walls forming the background to a magpie-like jumble of books, magazines, pictures and plants. If you have an interesting combination of pieces of furniture, you may find that they look most striking and effective when set against a neutral background. For a serene and elegant room, you could use soft tones of creams, buttermilks or pale greys, perhaps with accents of naturals such as soft smoky blue or earthy terracotta. You can also choose other looks: rustic simplicity, with coir matting, terracotta tiles and country furniture; high sophistication, with white walls, details picked out in black, metal curtain poles, modern furniture and abstract lines; or supreme elegance, with decorative wallpapers, richly textured fabrics and beautiful trimmings and details. Cherished collections of objects add style, emphasis and individuality to a neutrals room, whether they are assortments of china, photographs, pictures or other collectables.

Texture is a valuable element of any decorative scheme but it has a particular relevance when neutrals are involved since, in the absence of colour and pattern, the eye tends to be drawn to the texture. You can therefore begin to consider different kinds of texture, from hard, hairy, tweedy or knobbly on the one hand to soft, smooth, silky or lacy on the other. Ideally, try to contrast different textures, such as the rough, tough consistency of jute, in the form of sisal rugs, with the smooth, polished pale wood on which they might lie. Or you could contrast the translucency and smoothness of glass with the texture of a white-painted brick wall, perhaps. Large pebbles, washed smooth by the tide over thousands of years, make a wonderful contrast with the pale distempered surface of rough plaster in a window recess. A collection of old bottles can sit on a roughly-hewn wooden shelf. Lace panels can be sewn on to cushions, to create a welcome textural relief from the heavier, denser weaves of upholstery fabrics. These differences in texture bring interiors to life and although the effect is subtle, it is also extremely effective.

Texture

Texture is, quite often, the last element to be considered but it can make all the difference to the success, or otherwise, of any scheme. Combinations of textures that do not go together, or that are too similar, can create a disturbing atmosphere. Interiors that were popular in the 1950s, with all-pervasive smooth surfaces of plastic and glass, were sometimes cold and unfriendly to the point of alienation, particularly when combined with colours created from strong chemical dyes.

A neutral decor today is synonymous with a natural look. It is the textural contrasts that create this look, by copying the diversity of texture found in nature itself. Among the different textures available to the interior decorator, wood is one of the most rewarding surfaces of all. It introduces a considerable wealth of colour, texture and pattern to a room before any other element is added, and it also has warmth and character. The easiest and most common way to use wood in a neutrals room is through the furniture, which can range from elegant Regency or heavy Victorian to French country, painted Swedish or practical domestic furniture.

Many hardwoods, from which most furniture is made, have rich surface patterning and sometimes colour variation as well, from the intricately swirling patterns of walnut to the smooth simplicity and fine grain of beech or chestnut. Each wood has its own colour, from the deep reddish-brown of rosewood or mahogany to the golden yellow of maple. Part of a cabinet-maker's skill lies in creating designs that make the most of the wood's grain, texture and colour, and also in choosing a wood that suits the purpose for which it is intended. Expensive pieces of furniture are usually made from hardwoods and fruitwoods, perhaps with decorative veneers or inlays, while country furniture, such as dining tables and dressers, is often made from pine, which is an inexpensive softwood.

Many of the untreated woods, such as pine, chestnut, elm and beech, are fairly pale in their own right, but will darken with age indoors if not preserved in some way. To create paler wood surfaces without losing the character of the wood itself, you can opt for one of the white woodstains, which have now become very sophisticated in terms of both the products themselves and the range of colours they are supplied in. Many of them are water-based, which allows you to tint the wood with a matt, opaque finish that still permits the grain of the wood to show through. Alternatively, you can use liming wax or wash the wood in white paint which you then partly wipe off for an antiqued effect.

Paints The formulation of paint varies according to the manufacturer so, when planning a neutrals-based scheme, think carefully about the paint, since the sheen or lack of it will be crucially important in the final look. An old-fashioned distemper (which is based on lime), such as that supplied in the National Trust range of paints, will give a completely different look from a silk vinyl, particularly when there is no other colour around to distract the eye from the paint's finish.

Traditional paint formulations have a long local history, with the formula, and sometimes the colour, varying according to the pigments and minerals available. For example, the traditional stone houses of Wales and Greece, although very different in character, are painted in limewash which is an excellent paint to use for stone walls because, being porous, it allows the stone to breathe. The resulting paint is powdery and thin, therefore allowing the underlying texture of the walls to show through. Limewash is usually a simple mixture with no colour added, although pigments, particularly natural earth ones such as yellow ochre or burnt umber, can be added to it.

Magnolia and gardenia, both shades of off-white, are the two biggest-selling paint colours in Britain. This is because they are easy to live with and provide a good background for many different decorating and furniture styles. In addition, many people like them because they are warmer than pure white, which is very cold. However, the range of paints in neutral tones has expanded considerably in the last few years and there are now many more subtle options open to anyone wishing to decorate in neutrals.

As with colours, the bluer tones of white will seem colder, and the yellow or pink tones much warmer. If you find you have made the wrong choice, you can do a great deal to warm up a cool colour by altering the lighting. You can choose from halogen, fluorescent, daylight-effect, low-wattage and tinted bulbs, or atmospheric groups of candles, to create a variety of moods in a room and to soften or warm the decorative scheme, according to the effect you want to create.

This close-up of a pantry reveals the real joy of neutrals – the way in which texture plays such an important part, from the rough wicker of the basket to the smooth surface of the eggs, the translucent sheen of the glass jars and the almost papery texture of the vegetables. Light and shadow play a major role in creating this feeling of texture, and subtly different shades of colour – as shown in the toning cream paintwork – enhance it.

Papers

If you want a pattern, design, motif or texture on your walls, then paper is an excellent choice. The texture plays an important part in the overall look, whether you are using a thick, embossed paper or thin lining paper. There is a wealth of wallpaper designs that are more or less self-coloured, with only a small tonal variation between the pattern and the backing colour. If you find areas of plain paper or paint too stark, this type of paper would be an obvious choice. Self-stripes in cream and white look sophisticated without appearing cold in any way, and are suitable for most situations. Monotone wallpapers are tonal with simple designs, which give walls an interesting textural quality in subtle, neutral tones without overwhelming a room. Equally, large-print wallpapers which represent the designs of tonal damask fabrics are an ideal way to introduce pattern and decoration into a neutrals colour scheme, and are especially suitable for elegant and formal rooms. Geometric patterns or stripes tend to suit the modern idiom better than more ornate designs, although much depends on the architecture of the room and the style of the furnishings.

Fabrics

With fabric, texture really comes into its own. You have a rich and exciting variety of weaves, patterns and materials from which to choose, from heavy raised brocades to gossamer- thin voiles, from roughly woven tweeds to shimmery silks. The use of one colour makes the texture of the fabric its most outstanding quality, and much depends on the fibres used in its construction, as well as in the weight and sheen of the cloth. Among the fabrics suitable for neutrals schemes are those with a self-pattern, such as jacquards (which can have complex self-patterns) and dobbys (which have simple, geometric self-patterns). Epinglés, which are similar in texture to tapestry but have looser stitches, are ideal fabrics for neutrals schemes. Natural, unbleached linens are also extremely effective, as are pale florals which look as though they have been gently faded by the sun.

Fortunately for the home decorator, many of the simple neutral fabrics are inexpensive, because they are the unadorned, unrefined basic cloth. Calico is an example of this, with its tough, heavy-duty, matt character. It is one of the most popular natural, unbleached fabrics, and is particularly suitable for summer decorating – it can be used to make slip-covers for upholstered furniture that would otherwise look too hot in the summer. These covers can be removed when the weather starts to get cooler in the autumn. Originally used for lining grander fabrics, calico's serviceable qualities and sheer value for money have made it popular for a range of soft furnishings, particularly for the more architecturally-inspired types of blinds, such as roller or Roman blinds, and for simple, generously draped and dressed curtains. Entire rooms have been decorated in

calico, with draped bedheadings, swagged and dressed curtains, and simply designed chair covers. Combined with other neutral fabrics such as crisp white bedlinen and sisal rugs, calico creates a look that is both luxurious yet simple. One of the advantages of using a plain, neutral and inexpensive fabric such as this is that you can afford to buy enough of it to drape it extravagantly.

Other good choices for fabrics in a neutrals scheme are those with a strongly textured weave, such as linens, cotton reps and rich jacquard patterns in silk or wool, and loosely woven woollens and cottons. Slubby silks, like textured noils and tussers, react with the light to create marvellous patterns of highlight and shade. Linen union, a mixture of cotton and linen, makes an extremely tough fabric that is ideal for either upholstery or drapery, and comes in some wonderful, rich, neutral and natural colours, with interesting self-woven patterns or printed designs. Printed cottons and silks, in monochromatic colour combinations – greys, whites, beiges and blacks – also fit in well in this kind of interior, as do embroidered cottons in pale colours and simple ginghams for a Scandinavian look. One of the recent innovations is the introduction of crewelwork-style machine-embroidered fabrics, often in white or cream on a beige or pastel background. Large rooms can take more elaborate fabric patterns, and the use of drapery in

Texture plays an important role in this neutrals colour scheme, as does the mixture of delicately patterned fabrics. From the translucent folds of the curtain to the polished sheen of the boards and the rough surface of the woven jacquard used for some of the sofa and chair covers, texture helps to create visual interest in what would otherwise be a uniform colour scheme.

abundance will allow you more freedom with pattern, but beware of choosing patterns that are too bright and bold for the size of the room as they will be overwhelming.

Translucent fabrics – in the form of lace and voiles in whites, creams and beiges – are always popular, in particular for drapes, either set at the window or around a bed. The soft, sweeping lines of these fabrics give a room a romantic and sometimes mysterious atmosphere. Muslins, voiles, machine-made lace and fine silks have been employed for years as under-curtains or glass-cloths, hung on simple rods next to the window behind more ornate curtains. Today they are often used independently as bed hangings, an influence of the colonial empire and hot climates where they serve a very important function as mosquito netting. These fine fabrics sometimes look nice when contrasted with a heavier and more elaborate fabric, such as heavily patterned cotton, silk damask or linen, to give a rich, vibrant quality to the room.

Windows

Neutral colour schemes work very well for most windows, since they allow the attention to concentrate on the window itself. They are, therefore, best used to frame an already distinguished-looking window, in the same way that a picture frame can set off a painting. According to the style of the window and the feel of the room, the window dressing can be simple and unobtrusive or elaborate and decorative. Details which would not be seen on highly-patterned fabrics can be used to great advantage on curtains and drapes in neutrals colour schemes. For example, curtains in a neutrals room with a contemporary feel could be given pencil pleats or a simple tab heading, while those in a period room could be given swags and tails, or perhaps a pelmet cut into harlequin points or scallops. Trimmings are also very important in neutrals schemes, because they add depth, interest, detail and texture – you could arrange toning braids across the curtain headings, tie back the curtains with thick loops of cord or perhaps pipe the leading edge of the curtains in a different pattern or colour. You can also create interest by stitching together strips of complementary fabrics to make striped curtains.

Windows with handsome proportions, such as the elegant tall windows you find in Georgian houses, are often best left unadorned except for simple wooden shutters or perhaps a plain Holland blind in stiff canvas. Alternatively, Roman blinds in plain calico or London blinds – which have a simple drawstring mechanism – in a fine, plain white cotton weave fit neatly into any window that is taller than it is wide, and offset the proportions well. Roller or Roman blinds in wide, short windows can look wrong.

One of the other popular uses for neutral fabrics has been for translucent window-screens. Lace has traditionally been used for this purpose, and there are many new and

6 2

exciting ways to tackle the problem of privacy in a town house or flat without resorting to machine-made synthetic lace curtains. If you choose carefully, the window-screen becomes a stylish statement in its own right. Organdie – a form of crisp, stiff, muslin – can be used, hanging plain and unpleated from a simple pole, or a translucent version of the London blind can be constructed instead. Alternatively, antique pieces of lace can be draped over a pole so that they hang in folds.

Furniture and finishes

When planning the furniture for a neutrals scheme, you need to think carefully about shape as well as colour and texture. For most neutrals schemes, the emphasis is on space and light, so you need to ensure that the overall effect does not look cluttered or bitty. Large sofas and deep chairs, upholstered in pale, textured fabrics, look good combined with painted or stripped and waxed woods. You can create a wonderfully informal and relaxed mood by using furniture made from rattan, wicker and cane, or choosing Lloyd Loom chairs, sofas or low tables, especially if you combine them with plenty of plants. Sometimes, if the atmosphere and style of the room are appropriate, decorative elements such as pictures may look best if kept large and simply framed. If you opt for strong colour in the form of paintings or posters, check that they make a sufficient statement to warrant the intrusion of the colour, either by hanging them in close proximity to one another or repeating their colours and shapes elsewhere. Failure to do so will result in the painting or poster dominating the room, which may of course be your intention, especially if the painting is the focus for the entire room. Alternatively, if you do not want to introduce large splashes of colour, you can decorate the walls with an eclectic mix of small watercolours, engravings, antique maps or black and white photographs.

Flowers, too, need to be considered in this kind of setting. Massed displays of sculptural flowers in a single colour will enhance the neutrals theme of the room – big bowls of white or yellow tulips, perhaps, a large jug of white or pale blue hydrangeas, or a silver rose bowl filled with white or pale pink roses. A cottage-style display of different coloured flowers might be ideal for an informal room decorated in neutral or natural colours and filled with country furniture. Architectural houseplants, such as spiky palms, suit a sophisticated neutrals room and accentuate its clean lines, or you might wish to soften the atmosphere with huge pots of marguerites or frilly-leafed scented geraniums.

A neutrals scheme is excellent for displaying sculpture of almost any sort, enabling you to focus attention properly on the shape and texture of the piece. Whether your taste is for representational or abstract forms, positioning the sculpture carefully against a plain, unadorned background will make the most of it.

A Cream Kitchen

A neutrals and naturals theme was chosen for this large, light kitchen, in which the warm, glowing tones of wood are the major feature, for the floors, the kitchen cupboards and the work surfaces. It illustrates the point that when you remove colour from a decorating scheme, your eye automatically focuses on shape and texture. You notice, for example, the different colours in the wood itself, and the way that the grain runs. Details become important, and your eye is drawn to anything that stands out – be it the little painted cupboard, or the thick, soft folds of the hessian blind at the window – in which texture and shape instead of colour play a major feature. The old wooden beam above the window, with its irregular form, stands out both tonally and architecturally from the smoothness of the rest of the room, and its roughly hewn shape is echoed in the rough texture and unrodded folds of the blind beneath, its pulling mechanism, appropriately, being jute rope. It is also worth noting how well the blind fits below this beam, seeming to flow from it without interruption and with no visible heading.

Light plays a dominant role in this kind of scheme, since it is the play of light that reveals the shadows and highlights of the surfaces. During the day, it pours in through the windows while at night discreet spotlights in the ceiling perform a diffusing function. Since lighting creates mood and atmosphere, it is well worth ensuring that you choose well, particularly in a kitchen where some kind of dual-purpose lighting is required – bright light for the work areas, and a more subtle, diffused light for the parts of the room where you eat and relax.

A collection of old wooden chairs pick up the texture and antique feel of the wooden beams, their different outlines making a contrast of texture and shape with the paler colours and simple lines of the cupboards and table. Rough cream hessian chair cushions have been tied in position with natural rope – an echo of the texture which has been used for the blind mechanism.

In a scheme like this, even the kitchen utensils have been carefully considered, and are in the neutrals theme. Although this might seem purist, small splashes of bright or disparate colours would distract the eye, and spoil the impression that this room makes. One of the advantages of opting for this sort of neutrals scheme in a kitchen is that it focuses interest on the activities that take place within the room, and the people that use it. Since kitchens are, in many houses, the heart of the home, this is a particularly successful concept for decorating because it gives the kitchen something of the intimate feel of a Vermeer painting. Colour, if required, could be provided in the form of a large noticeboard for children's drawings and for favourite postcards and wrappers, as well as the more mundane paperwork that invariably accompanies family life.

OPPOSITE *This small, antique meat-safe has been painted cream, and the door frame decorated with a design of different vegetables, in natural colours. Although this has been hand-painted, a similar design could be created with stencils.*

A neutrals colour theme works well for kitchens, particularly where, as here, natural wood has been used for almost all the surfaces, creating a rich interplay of texture and soft, pale colour. The cream Aga fits seamlessly into the overall scheme, its traditional curved lines in keeping with the old wooden beams, further echoed by the different shapes of the kitchen chairs. Textural contrast is provided by the natural hessian blind, the chair cushions and their rope ties. No strong colour intrudes on this scheme.

Subtle shifts of pale tone are the keynotes of this elegant Swedish-style dining room. Simple lines and a monochrome colour scheme play an important part in the calm atmosphere, creating a wonderful feeling of space and light. Note how the detailing around the cornices in a deeper greyish-white helps to define the shape of the room and draws attention to the architecture. The Gustavian look is one of purity of line, restrained elegance, light, simple, cool colours and a balanced arrangement of the furniture. This room has been kept simple, but sometimes the look is highly decorated.

A Swedish-style Dining Room

Loosely based on what is known as the Gustavian style, this dining room is elegant yet simple. It relies on the natural beauty of wood, delicately washed in pastel tones, so can be translated successfully to both town and country houses. At first glance, the room appears to be monochromatic and simple, with a minimal colour scheme based on tones of off-whites and greys. However, a closer look reveals the elegance of the decoration and the wealth of delicate details, making this a sophisticated and serene scheme for an English country dining room. It has been designed around the elegant Swedish dining table and chairs, which are painted in a pale dove grey. The detailing in the room is rich in different textures and patterns, and a range of neutral colours has been used for the curtains and chair covers, the painted furniture, the collections of glass and pewter, the table linen and the china.

The original Scandinavian Gustavian style derives from the period of King Gustav III of Sweden in the eighteenth century, its hallmark being a purity of line, softened by the addition of pearly-grey, blue, cream or white paint. It is the determination to paint every item of furniture which typifies the Scandinavian look, as much as the colours used, in particular the painting of the simple softwood boarded floors, which also helps to create the 'clean' style. Much of the paint used in Scandinavia contains lime. This was the original preservative used in paint both in Northern Europe and elsewhere before modern chemicals took its place. The lime adds both a chalkiness and a luminosity to the finished effect and it is this subtle combination of opacity with sheen, often allowing some of the natural wood finish beneath to show through, that creates the final look.

Precisely because it is subtle and pale, you have to be extremely careful how you deal with the rest of the colour palette in the room. In Scandinavian schemes, a particular soft palette of blue, grey, ochre, Indian red (red oxide) and occasionally yellow and a soft viridian is used. The key is to ensure that no single colour dominates or stands out too sharply against the others, otherwise the look is lost.

This colour palette is used in Scandinavian rooms which receive cold north light, because the pale colours increase the amount of light in the room – a very important consideration in a climate where the winter days are extremely short. Painting over the wood introduces yet more light-reflective surfaces into the room and also helps to make relatively cheap softwoods look much smarter. In addition, the white paint picks up colour from the underlying wood, a process which is often helped along by adding a little washed-down ochre and Indian red to the paint. The shade of blue used is important – it must contain enough yellow to be warm, without so much that it moves towards the greener end of the blue spectrum.

OPPOSITE *Pewter has a rich and wonderfully lustrous appearance. Its soft grey sheen blends well with many different colour combinations but is shown off to great advantage against this distressed painted shelf. The solid, simple shapes combined with the reflectivity of the metal work particularly well in a restrained neutrals scheme.*

Painting the floorboards

There are various ways of creating pale-coloured wooden floors. Much depends on the surface that exists already. You can, if you wish, lime an ordinary wooden floor using liming wax or paste, which will very effectively remove the 'orange' look of a pine floor, for example. For this floor, which was already stained a fairly dark colour, and had a paler centre where a carpet had once been, a simple colourwash painted look was applied, which kept this change of tone intact.

you will need　Sandpaper • Clear matt acrylic varnish • White pigment • Straight edge • Masking tape • Dove grey paint

1 Clean and lightly sand down the existing surface of the floor to remove any grease and to provide a key for the paint.

2 Using a mixture of acrylic varnish and white pigment, which has been well diluted with water, brush this on to the floor in one or two coats to soften the stained areas and make them look paler.

3 Use a straight edge to draw the lines for the double border on the floor. Using these marks as a guide, run three lines of masking tape, about 2.5 cm (1 in) apart from each other, a little way in from the skirting boards all round the room.

4 Carefully paint between the lines of masking tape with a small roller or brush, using a pale dove grey paint. Leave to dry, then apply a thin coat of varnish to seal the paintwork.

Curtains with border

Simplicity is the keynote of these elegant curtains bordered with the same woven jacquard fabric in a contrasting colour. Make lined curtains in the usual way, and follow the instructions here to add a border down the leading edges and along the lower edges prior to attaching the lining. The complete border is assembled, and the corner at the lower edge where the two pieces meet is mitred, before the border is joined to the curtain. The instructions are for one curtain.

you will need   Curtain fabric and lining • Contrasting fabric for border • Sewing thread

1 For each curtain, cut one 20 cm (8 in) wide strip to the width of the curtain plus 11.5 cm (4⅝ in), and one 20 cm (8 in) wide strip to the length of the curtain plus 11.5 cm (4⅝ in). Fold the strips in half lengthwise, wrong sides together, and press. Now fold one end of the side border strip diagonally so that the end is even with the pressed fold; press and cut along this pressed diagonal fold. Unfold the strip: you should have an outward-pointing V-shape. Do this to one end of the lower border strip as well.

2 With the strips unfolded and placed with their right sides together, join the pointed end of the side border to the pointed end of the lower border, taking a 1.5 cm (⅝ in) seam allowance, and stopping the stitching at each side 1.5 cm (⅝ in) from the edge. Carefully trim the seam and corner with a pair of sharp scissors, then turn the border right side out. Press the seam open.

3 With right sides together and raw edges even, position the border on the curtain. Clip into the seam allowance of the border at the mitred corner so it lies flat. Pin and stitch, with a 1.5 cm (⅝ in) seam allowance. Stitch into the mitred corner (rather than beginning the stitching there). Press the extra fabric of the border out of the way.

4 Press the border away from the main curtain. Now line the curtains in the usual way, making sure that you cover with the lining the raw edges of the seam which joins the curtain to the border.

Taking pride of place in the centre of the dining table is a Wedgwood creamware tureen. Originally designed for 'below stairs' use as functional china, its elegant simplicity has turned it into a valuable collector's item. It symbolizes the purity of colour, line and texture that is at the heart of any neutrals scheme.

Introducing light and texture

OPPOSITE BOTTOM *An antique chest has been painted and distressed in a shade of dark greyish-green, with the cream paint picking out the detailing. The silvery-grey pewter plates and greyish-green foliage and cream flowers in a tall glass vase unify the colour scheme.*

The paints used in this room have been carefully chosen from the National Trust range of historic paints to bring as much light into the room as possible, yet they are all earthy, soft shades of white instead of harsh, brilliant white. Instead of painting the room in one or two colours, four shades of off-white have been used to create interest and atmosphere. Lime white, which is the same shade as soft white limewash or distemper, covers the walls. Old white is used for the ceiling; off-white for the glazing bars on the windows; and a neutral, greyish-white on the skirting boards and the architraves around the windows and doors. These four paint shades work well together, add depth and focus to the colour scheme and create a subtle effect simply because they are all based on white, rather than being white tinted with a slight colour.

The floor is also painted to continue the Swedish theme, and step-by-step instructions on how this is done are given on pages 72–3. There are many different methods for painting floors, and just as many different effects that can be achieved. However, in a Gustavian scheme, the aim is not to create a solid, opaque layer of colour but to consider the floor as part of the entire scheme. In this room, some of the floor was originally black and so needed careful treatment which would allow the dark stain to show through without being the most dominant feature.

The sheen, life and character provided by the bleached floor, coupled with the sunlight flooding in from the window, are what give this room its vitality. It cannot be over-emphasized how important this quality is in interior decorating, no matter how well you mix and match the colours, because without it a room will appear to be flat and uninteresting.

A muted, greyish-green has been added as a subtle accent colour in the room to give the neutral tones something to bounce off. The leading edges of the curtains have heath green borders, and this green also appears in the thin stripe of the chair covers, the gingham lampshade in the corner, the collection of glasses arranged in the window, and the plants and greenery in the garden outside.

It is not just colour that provides atmosphere, but colour coupled with texture and the way the light plays on, reflects and absorbs colour. As discussed on pages 56–8, texture is not a fixed item – we perceive it only through light and the interplay of light with it, and in decorating this is a key element in choosing and combining colours.

As with all neutrals schemes, texture plays an important part in the success of this room's decoration. There are several clever uses of it, including the wide variety of linen on the table. The delicate white cotton tablemats and small lace mats for the glasses add a splash of white to the table; beige linen mats pick out the taupe colour of the chair covers and are carefully arranged to create intriguing layers of different textures on the table top. The carving on the side of the table and the lovely quality of peeling paint also add to this. The silver on the dining table and the collection of antique pewter plates bring a metallic quality to the scheme as well as extending the grey tones of the painted furniture. Antique, classic Wedgwood creamware adds the sophisticated texture of smooth, reflective porcelain and picks up the warm, creamy colour of the curtains. The collection of glass plates on the large window introduce pattern, the line of antique wine glasses on the smaller window contain splashes of the heath green seen elsewhere in the dining room, and both add a translucent texture which brings a further luminous quality into the decorative scheme.

ABOVE *This table setting shows a subtle variety of pale tones and layers of different textures – from the painted distressed wood of the table, through the delicate worked threads of the white and cream embroidered table linen, and the smoothness of the silver and glassware.*

LEFT *With their deep shadows and brilliant highlights, the papery pure white flowers of these hydrangeas in a simple cream bowl demonstrate how pale colours reflect and absorb light. Even white is never all one tone – it changes with the quality of light.*

RIGHT *A collection of clear and green antique wine glasses, in a variety of shapes, stands on a window ledge where the light will catch it, and show the translucency of the glass off to perfection. In a similar way, a collection of glass ice plates has been arranged on another window ledge (see page 76).*

Fabric

To keep the typically Swedish quality of restrained elegance and concentrate the scheme on colour and texture rather than pattern, a lightweight woven jacquard which is the colour of unbleached cotton has been chosen for the curtains. The fabric has the textural quality of damask, which gives elegance to the room, and its creamy colour brings warmth. The curtains hang from an ordinary track on a simple heading and have been edged with a wide heath green strip of the same fabric around the leading edge and along the drop (see pages 74–5 for instructions on how to do this), and allowed to pool slightly on the floor. There is no room here for a pelmet or even any fancy heading but a decorative feature has been made of the window by arranging a collection of antique glass plates on one window and green glass on another. The chairs have been covered in a woven ticking with narrow stripes of taupe, white and heath green.

CHAPTER 3

yellows

The colour of sunshine, yellow is one of the most uplifting and versatile colours to use in decoration. Ranging as it does from the palest of lemons, warm sunny cowslip, bright mustard and egg yolk to rich, earthy ochres, golds and other exotic Eastern shades, yellow contains a vast range of shades. It can be the colour of the pale primroses and buttery cowslips of spring; of abundant summer flowers such as irises, roses, lilies and sunflowers; of fields of straw, hay and corn in high summer – associations which have made the colour a big success for Laura Ashley. It can be the rich, uninhibited, butter and mustard yellows of Provence and the Mediterranean; the elegant golds of royal palaces; or the spicy yellows of saffron and turmeric.

Yellow is a wonderful colour for decoration. For a cold house which gets little sunshine, yellow can exact a transformation. Even adding a little yellow to a cold house painted in a harsh white can turn it into something much more welcoming. For those who want a bolder statement, rich, sunny yellows can be used as paint or paper on the walls, to give the effect of drenching the room in sunshine.

Yellow, being such a naturally bright colour, has the capacity to startle and surprise, and it is worth exploiting its slightly eccentric quality. However, it can be difficult to find the right shade for a particular room. The yellow you first choose might be too sharp, too acid, too cold or too orange, so it is worth testing out as large an area of the colour as you can find before committing yourself. Nevertheless, once you have found the exact shade, you will no doubt be delighted with it. You can also mix yellow with other colours – cowslip combined with sapphire is an extremely successful combination for Laura Ashley. Increase the impact by introducing bold colour combinations such as bright, china blue or scarlet which, when used with a similarly saturated egg yolk yellow, make a warm, very vibrant scheme; or use soft blues, whites or greys for a pale scheme.

Since yellow is one of the colours of sunshine, it is important to consider its contribution to the overall scheme. The existing colour of any scheme can be subtly and sometimes even substantially altered by the colour and tone of the light that falls on it, whether artificial or real. This means that not only can you compensate for a hard, cold, naturally blue light by using naturally warm yellow tones in the paintwork and fabrics, but so too can you use yellow-toned light.

Historical associations

Yellow was not used very much by interior decorators in the past, although it was favoured by artists such as Van Gogh, Monet and the Bloomsbury Group who liked its surprising and dashing qualities. It was also associated with royalty – Oriental emperors liked Chinese yellow, and a deeper shade was the favourite colour of Louis XIV, the Sun

King of France. Yellow's association with gold has always made it seem both rich and exotic. Until the 1820s, when the more acidic, greenish, chrome yellow was first manufactured cheaply, most of the yellows used relied on the earth pigments of yellow ochre and raw sienna that occur naturally in different parts of the world.

One of the bravest uses of yellow was in Sir John Soane's drawing room at his house in Lincoln's Inn Fields, London, which relies on an almost unrelieved use of brilliant chrome yellow for both paintwork and fabrics. Unusually, the contrast to the yellow is a deep crimson, used to edge the silk curtains and to braid the upholstery. This is clever because the choice of red warms the acidity of the yellow and gives it more vibrancy.

More modern enthusiasts of decorating with yellow have been painters like Monet at his house in Giverny, France, and Duncan Grant and Vanessa Bell at Charleston in East Sussex. Monet's famous all-yellow dining room at Giverny uses a mid, bright blue as a contrast for the fabric and ceramics. Yellow was used at Charleston and one of Duncan Grant's own designs from the 1930s, the primrose yellow and pale grey Grapes fabric (reintroduced by Laura Ashley in 1987) hangs in the garden room. A warmer yellow has also been used, with great panache, as the background colour to the English country house style of decorating in the second half of the twentieth century, using several shades of the same hue to create an unparalleled feeling of reflectivity and life. Yellow was also popular in the 1950s and 1960s, when primary colours were so fashionable.

If you want to see a bold use of yellow, the drawing room at Sir John Soane's house in London is a perfect example. A wonderfully bold chrome yellow has been used for both the walls and the magnificent silk curtains, which are bordered in deep crimson. The yellow is a brilliant contrast for the dark wooden furniture. Even the polished wooden floor has a strong yellowish tinge, no doubt reflecting yellow from the rest of the room.

Lemon yellow   The sharp, light, slightly acidic tones of lemon yellow can look marvellous in big, sunny modern rooms, accompanied by natural fabrics such as cottons or rustic, woven cloths. It is equally beautiful in silk, for an elegant, formal look. Lemon yellow can be combined successfully with a sharp lime green and white, or contrasted with a deep, warm blue which neutralizes the acidity and gives the whole scheme a softer, more gentle appearance. In a scheme where florals are used, it can be combined with other light colours, such as blues, greens and apricots, to create a modern, country house look using bleached wood furniture, perhaps, and stripped floors. Historically, lemon yellow was popular in the Empire period and again in the nineteenth century (see Sir John Soane's dining room on page 83). In very recent times, it has been combined, in a slightly warmer, more primrose-like tone, with pale grey which, like the blue, tends to remove the acidity but, unlike the blue, leaves a much cooler-looking scheme. It is also used as an ice-cream sorbet colour, often combined with pistachio green and hot pink.

Butter yellow   The warmer, buttery yellows – colours often called cowslip, straw, buttercup or sunflower yellow – are very versatile and easy to live with. They are ideal colours for country prints, and create a wonderful sense of relaxation because they can evoke the soft, gentle sunshine of a spring day in Britain or, in more vibrant shades, the warmth of Provence. These yellows tend to enhance almost any space – whether it is a kitchen, bathroom, living room or bedroom – because they can be paired with a whole range of other colours. They are particularly effective for wall colours, and combine well with a wide range of colours, such as clear blues, deep burgundy reds and mid-toned greens, and are given crispness when combined with white.

Yellow ochre   Surprisingly, this dull, earthy yellow is also a versatile decorating colour. It has a similar colour palette to butter yellows, and was influenced by the colours of the East – saffron, turmeric, mustard and ochre. Its dullness provides an excellent contrast for brighter hues such as turquoise, Indian red, electric-blue and even some shades of pink. Yellow ochre is particularly valuable for achieving antiqued or distressed effects in paintwork. It frequently appears in Persian tile patterns, when it is often combined with cobalt blue and Indian red. It is also used in Europe, where the colour occurs naturally in the earth in the form of ochre and sienna pigments.

Gold   This is one of the most popular accent colours to be used in the decorative arts because it enhances all sorts of room schemes, whether in the form of simple gilding on mirrors and

The sharply curving outlines of the fine antique creamware contrast with the softly billowing shapes of the orange and gold parrot tulips. The decorated plates in the background link both the colour and form of the flowers and china.

picture frames, on edgings and mouldings, items made from brass, or in the gold lacquered furniture of the Louis XIV period. Gold, and muted old gold, can also be used in fabrics, such as those made by Fortuny, Genoese velvets and Venetian damasks. Gold adds an unmistakable touch of luxury and elegance to any room, but has to be handled with great care to ensure it looks distinguished. When combined with deep, rich colours such as red, purple, deep green and deep blue, gold has a very regal appearance, reminiscent of exotic Eastern palaces.

Orange-yellow

This colour ranges from the palest pastel apricot, through warm and rich marmalade-yellow to bright, primary orange. These shades can either be subtle, pale and soft, adding just a hint of warmth to a white base, or they can be strident, strong colours that demand attention. The soft apricot shades are very easy to work with and blend well with blues, greens and greys, making an excellent background to the patina and depth of colour of any of the woods with reddish tones.

Texture

Texture is important in yellow colour schemes because the interplay of light and dark on shades of yellow can give dramatic effects. It is a very responsive colour for paint effects – matt textures can be used or broken paint effects, such as colourwashing, sponging or stippling over other colours. Applied as a transparent glaze, either in acrylics or oil paints, over a white ground (or indeed over existing white-painted walls), the effect will be light, bright and fresh. Applied over a darker tone – such as deeper shades of beige or light brown – the effect will be deep and warm, bringing to life the background colour (a technique which is often seen in Tuscany). This look works well when much paler neutrals are chosen for the fabrics, with the odd spot of brighter, richer colour –

Yellow can be warm or cool. In this room, the walls have been colourwashed in ochre, and the curtains have an apricot design on a yellow background.

terracottas and mid-blues, perhaps – acting as a contrast. Brilliant yellows can also be used with more sober colours, to pick out details – architraves, window frames, chair and picture rails, and cornices. Walls can be divided to allow one part to be painted plain bright yellow, while the upper part, above a chair rail, is papered in yellow and white checks or candy stripes, for example.

When bright and sunny, yellow translates best to surfaces which are reflective. It works well for walls, but has to be used with more care for furniture, although pieces painted in antiqued yellow ochre can look very successful, particularly if their borders are picked out in deep red or olive green. With the use of gold, all sorts of shiny and silky textures are possible, and rich gold braids, gilt-framed mirrors and paintings, and gilded furniture all add a touch of glamour and ornamentation to a room. Gold and gilt finishes need to be handled with care because they can sometimes be overpowering and fussy. They tend to look best when used sparingly, or in surprising places. One large, gilded item in what is otherwise a fairly plain room can look striking and stylish,

A cool citrus yellow has been used for these walls. The sofa fabric contains no yellow, and is patterned in green and terracotta. Avoiding repeating colours too slavishly, but picking ones that harmonize instead, creates a relaxed, lived-in feel to the room.

particularly when contrasted with plain fabrics, simple furniture and pale, waxed wood.

For a rich, opulent look, choose silks, damasks, brocades and velvets in the more golden shades of yellow; for fresh, summery appeal, choose yellow cottons in reps, sailcloths and cambrics. Yellow is one of the more popular colours in Far Eastern textile design, and is often a background colour in saris, for example, so it is worth looking in ethnic shops for bright yellow silks.

Furniture and decorative objects can also introduce a textured yellow theme to a room. Rattan furniture, straw baskets and hats, glazed yellow ceramic tiles and terracotta urns with their rims dipped in yellow glaze are all ideal.

Fabrics

Yellow is a particularly suitable colour for fabric, especially as a background colour for other patterns or an accent colour for floral designs. Along with pink, yellow is one of the most popular colour motifs in floral patterns of all descriptions. An extensive range of yellow-based patterns is available, from small sprigged country motifs to big blowzy cabbage rose designs, most of them combined with green and blue. Provençal cotton uses wonderful deep, rich yellows, in floral and geometric patterns, mixed with bright blues and deep reds, for a sophisticated patterned effect. Often these brilliantly printed fabrics do not contain any white, and it is this depth of strong colour, combined with yellow, that gives them their characteristic intensity and charm.

English country house florals are available in a marvellously varied range of patterns, often with birds, insects and flowers. They frequently contain dull shades of gold and yellow, combined with mid-greens, blues and pinks. They can look particularly effective when the colours are subdued and appear to have been faded by the sun, or years of use.

When choosing a suitable fabric, much depends on the depth of colour in the yellow itself. For the gold end of the spectrum, you have the opportunity to plump for damasks,

OPPOSITE *Cowslip yellow combines particularly well with chambray blue in this drawing room, which shows a variety of yellow floral chintzes. White, used here for the colourwashed boards, helps to lift the overall colour scheme and give it a lighter feel, in an interesting twist to the normal decorating idiom where the boards are generally dark and the furniture pale. The patchwork quilt on the wall provides a decorative and unusual backdrop.*

Yellow decorative details

dobbys, brocades, rich silks and opulent crushed velvets, which are used mainly for their reflective and luminous qualities. If you move towards the more lemony yellows, then simple, natural fabrics – linens and cottons – are ideal because they enhance the fresh attributes of these shades, as do silks and chintzes. On the whole, the more acid yellows, which contain plenty of green, lend themselves to clean, crisp fabrics – sharp cottons, for example, or glazed chintzes. Yellow and white make a good clear mixture in ginghams, candy-striped cottons, sailcloths and canvases, and yellows, plums, and deep blues mix well in rich floral patterns where white is excluded. Yellows and greens make fresh, light gardenesque prints. Old gold and ruby red are used in many exotic, Far Eastern fabrics and patterns; Turkish and Moorish designs combine saffron and cobalt blue.

Yellow provides a more interesting contrast for deep colours than white, and can be used in small ways to bring a colour scheme, based on these rich colours, to life. Cushions, tie-backs, braiding and piping in bright, buttery yellows work particularly well with deep blues and greens. You can contrast these colours with Victorian crimson for a strong scheme, in richly woven and highly patterned fabrics. For an Italian Renaissance look, consider mixing yellow with terracotta on figured grounds, such as damask or brocade. Gold braid and tassels can transform relatively simple curtains and drapes into something much grander, as can gilding a curtain pole (see pages 186–7), the edges of a piece of painted furniture, a lampstand or a photo frame.

Yellow is one of the strongest colours in nature's repertoire, much used by plants for attracting insects for the purpose of pollination. Yellow flowers can sing out in any room, from great armfuls of spring flowers, such as daffodils or tulips, to the wonderfully strong architectural shapes of sunflowers, so beloved of Van Gogh, whose love of yellow was second to none. As a change from flowers, bowls of yellow fruits can look stunning. You could mix lemons with limes for a sharp contrast, fill a low wooden bowl with honey-coloured pears or, in a contemporary room, use exotic yellow fruits such as star fruits and honey melons which have unusual shapes. Other details could include china, chosen to complement the style of the room. A country-style sitting room could show off a collection of plates with bright yellow borders and central floral patterns, while a yellow kitchen might be decorated with rustic yellow-glazed Mediterranean earthenware.

Walls and fabrics can be stamped or stencilled (see page 199) – try gold on white, on navy blue or on crimson for a rich contrast. You could cover the whole of a wall with an antique patchwork quilt which is predominantly yellow, or display a collection of yellow paintings, perhaps with a common, linking theme.

This light, well-proportioned room in a converted barn has a wealth of interesting architectural features – exposed beams, a beautiful wooden floor and the bonus of attractive views through the windows. A simple decorating scheme such as this one, which uses flat expanses of plain colour, helps to focus interest on the architectural features while keeping the sense of light and space.

A Yellow & White Living Room

OPPOSITE *Here you can see the deep, egg yolk yellow piping on the sofa arms and box cushions. It makes an excellent, subtle but clear contrast with the slub weave of the off-white sofa fabric. The yellow theme is picked up in one of the painted cushions, with a pattern that incorporates blue and green as well, and a piped blue border. A plain green cushion makes a simple, strong counterfoil to the painted design.*

A large, light room is a joy to decorate, provided you take account of the architectural features and create a scheme that enhances rather than works against them. This is a room in a converted barn on the East Anglian coast, and it is decorated for the relaxed simplicity of a family weekend retreat. The windows look out to sea, and it is an ideal room for easy, summer living.

Yellow was chosen for its warmth, and white was added to create lightness. The colours are kept as solid blocks to enhance the modernity of the barn, and the only pattern used is in the woven ticking stripe for an armchair and the painted cushions and curtains. These were hand-painted in a deliberately simple, almost abstract, design to continue the contemporary feel of the room.

By using pale cowslip yellow and white, with touches of sky blues and sea greens, the light and airy atmosphere is accentuated in this sunny, seaside room. The pale bleached wood of the polished floors and the roof timbers requires a simple decorative scheme that allows you to appreciate its natural beauty, texture and tone rather than be distracted by other details. The overall effect is similar to the bleached appearance of driftwood, which is appropriate as this house is situated close to the sea.

The choice of yellow for the walls has helped to add a touch of warmth, and the texture and consistency of the paint is also an important factor in this. A flat, dense paint that absorbs light will counteract any coldness, while looking and feeling warm. The yellow walls are an inspired choice: they offer the simplicity and straightforwardness of white or off-white, but cut down the glare which might otherwise be present in such a large room with so much glass.

Off-white has been chosen for the largest item of furniture in the room – the three-seater traditional sofa – and yellow has been used for the piping. This subtle and understated contrast works extremely well and is an idea that is well worth copying. The yellow piping provides the necessary outline without becoming too prominent, so it adds sculptural shape to the piece of furniture without distracting the eye from its overall form. Sea green and sky blue are both used as accent colours, seen in the paints used for the curtains and cushions, their contrast piping and as solid blocks of colour on the two upright chairs and plain cushions.

Plain-coloured, textured weaves and simple geometric stripes help to create the contemporary and very relaxed feel of this room. The cushions and the leading edges of the curtains have been hand-painted. Inexpensive calico, often used for linings, is an ideal fabric for painting, being both solid and dense enough to provide the equivalent of the artist's canvas. An alternative is the thick Indian cotton which is used here. You can

OPPOSITE *The far end of the same yellow room reveals an unexpectedly deep colour – a rich, warm mid-blue – painted on a curved wall which continues the line of the corridor. Although the room does not require this contrast, it is nevertheless a bonus and well worth copying in a similarly L-shaped room, or large alcove. Make sure that the contrasting colour ties in, as this does, with the decoration of the whole room, otherwise the effect may be jarring. Solid blocks of contrasting colour are working here with the positioning of the plain green chair against the blue wall and the solid yellow chair with two cushions, one in plain blue and one in plain green.*

RIGHT *Simple, well-constructed wooden furniture fits very well with this decorative scheme which is equally simple. The modern, clean lines of the table reflect the style of the room's architecture. If you are unable to match your furniture to the colour scheme in this way, you could paint the furniture – even inexpensive items can be made to marry with a scheme if painted in suitable colours.*

use ordinary emulsion paint or artist's acrylics for the painting. If you keep to a simple motif and a repeating design, you do not need the talent of Picasso to create surprisingly good results. Instructions for painting the cushions are given on pages 96–7.

If you wish to experiment with the colour scheme, it would be easy to take its principal features and reverse them, painting the walls green or blue, with a yellow alcove or recessed area (see opposite), using a yellow and white, or blue and white, striped fabric, and so on. A simple colour palette of four colours, of which two are the principal performers and two the chorus or background, is a good basis for a decorative scheme. If the colours are even in tone, as they are here with the exception of the white, they will give a sense of uniformity and tranquillity to the scheme. Tonal contrast will create a stronger, more dramatic impression.

Painting the cushions

Fabric can be painted in much the same way that any other surface is painted, but to prevent the paint from spreading and running you can size the fabric with a coat of diluted PVA first. You can use fabric paints, acrylic paints or ordinary household emulsion paint, all of which are washable, provided you handwash the fabric with care and do not wring or tumble-dry it. Use any simple design that takes your fancy; stripes, wavy lines, circles, triangles or spots. The paint does not have to adhere uniformly to the fabric – part of the charm of this design is its unevenness.

you will need Fabric (natural fibres and light colours are easiest) • Contrasting fabric, for piping • Piping cord • Sewing thread • Zip, 5 cm (2 in) less than size of cushion • PVA (optional) • Fabric paints, acrylic paints or emulsion paints • Cushion pad • Sewing machine with zip foot

1 Prepare the fabric by laying it on a board or waterproof surface, and stretch it taut, marking out with architect's tape the area for the painted design. Start to create the design using acrylic paints and a medium-sized artist's brush. It is most effective to work freehand, but if you are unsure of your painting skills you can practise on a spare piece of fabric first.

2 If you use more than one colour, keep a separate brush for each colour, and finish painting one colourway before adding the next. It is best to let the first colour dry completely before applying the second if the panels of colour will touch one another. This avoids the colours bleeding into each other. If using fabric paints, fix them according to the manufacturer's instructions.

3 Cut out the front and back of the cushion, leaving a 1.5 cm (⅝ in) seam allowance all round. Cut out 5 cm (2 in) wide strips of green fabric on the bias, and join together with diagonal seams until they fit the circumference of the cushion. Wrap the strips over the piping cord and machine baste next to the cord. Lay the piping along the seamline of the cushion front, with the cord facing inwards. Stitch in place. Clip into the seam allowance of the piping at the corners so the piping will go round the corners smoothly.

4 Place the open zip, face down, on the piping along the bottom edge of the cushion front and align the teeth with the stitching. Tack. Stitch through the zip tape and piping seam allowance, 3 mm (⅛ in) from the teeth. Turn under both seam allowances and close the zip so the folded edge meets the piping over the zip. Tack, then stitch 6 mm (¼ in) from the folded edge. Stitch across both ends of the zip up to the piping. With right sides together and zip open, stitch the two cushion pieces together. Clip corners, turn right sides out and press.

This bedroom has been painted in four shades of yellow to create a subtle interplay of light and shade which emphasizes its quirky architecture. A collection of straw hats continues the yellow theme. Hints of greens, browns, aquas, soft blues and ochres can be seen in the valance and quilt, and ochre yellow and smoky turquoise blue have been picked out for trimming the bedlinen. The decorative gilded lamp base and mirror add a further golden glow to the room.

A Yellow Bedroom

This large, square bedroom has been given an almost uniformly yellow colour scheme, but one with a difference – what might appear at first glance to be one yellow is actually several shades of one hue. The shades of yellow which have been chosen are particularly subtle and very warm, created from a soft earthy shade of yellow ochre blended with white, and together they create interest and add light and shade to the room. The simple colour scheme is almost Shaker-like in its appeal, although it is warmed by the varied patterns of the antique quilt on the bed, the pretty floral linen of the valance, and the rich variety of textures, including old pine, wicker, straw, sisal and the peeling, creamy paint on the head and foot of the bed. The scheme is kept light, fresh and feminine with the sprigged white voile curtains and the yellow check blind.

Simplicity is the keynote of this scheme, and as a result the architectural interest of the room's sloping ceilings is emphasized. The effect is both warm and light, which is particularly useful in a bedroom such as this which has relatively small windows, and the yellow glows from the sunlight streaming in.

Four different shades of yellow were chosen from the National Trust paint range. Three separate shades of yellow were painted on the walls, a pale yellow on the skirting boards, and cream on the ceiling. The four shades are an early nineteenth-century hay yellow which is bright but not excessively hot; a bright straw; a bright earthy cane colour which originated in Italy; and the yellow used by John Fowler for the staircase at Sudbury Hall, Derbyshire. A different shade has been used for each wall to create a lovely tonal effect of the various yellows working together to give atmosphere and light. These slightly earthy, muted, dusty yellows combine beautifully with the old gold-coloured linen in the room and look marvellous in old country houses.

If you are going to opt for a simple, painted scheme like this one, the quality and texture of the paint is extremely important because the way it reflects or absorbs light will affect the colour and warmth of the whole room. Paint should be chosen with care. For this room, paints with the texture of distemper were used instead of shiny acrylic. These matt paints look very effective on the surface of old plaster walls. Therefore, it pays to spend a little more time and money choosing not only the right colour of paint, but the appropriate type for the job. Always do a small test on one corner of the wall first to check that you like both the colour and finish.

If you wanted to create a little more decoration in this kind of scheme, stamping a very subtle pattern on the walls, perhaps in a dusty toning blue or green, would be very effective without altering the simple, country-style appeal, but beware of using too much pattern if you want to focus attention on the architectural detail.

Fabrics

A major feature of this room is the beautifully worked patchwork quilt. The paisley on top of the quilt features a mixture of yellows, beiges, browns, whites and greys, which contrast with plains and stripes on the underside in a range of complementary colours. Sometimes, old quilts were made from men's shirts as a practical way of using up discarded clothing; these were once known as 'strippies' in the North of England. Some quilts in England and Wales were made from Victorian dress fabrics whose designs have become a source of print design today. Quilts are wonderful heirlooms and a beautiful, antique quilt like this one can act as a starting point to a whole decorative scheme if you pick out a couple of key colours for the walls and curtains. You can quite easily re-create these quilts today with a sewing machine, using a combination of stripes and checks. Many of these old quilts were plain on one side and patterned on the other, and were quilted using attractive scrolling patterns, some of which were traditional and had been passed down from generation to generation. These, too, can be worked using a sewing machine, and many informative books are available on the subject. When making up a quilt of this kind, decide whether to opt for toning or contrasting colours and then plan the design accordingly. Be careful not to combine bright and subtle colours, as the brights will stand out far too vividly and spoil the uniform nature of the quilt.

The other fabrics in the room include the floral linen valance around the bed, which picks up the golds and creams in the rest of the room, and also appears as a cushion on the antique wooden chair. The cowslip check blind continues the yellow theme and the white voile curtains add light and a soft, fresh touch.

LEFT *Mixing two different kinds of fabric at the windows adds textural interest to the decorative scheme. The sheer voile curtains have been hung from a yellow-painted pole with wooden rings, with small ties decorating the points where the curtain heading is fixed to the rings themselves. The voile is the decorative element, and the blind is the practical window covering – a reversal of the normal practice.*

RIGHT *A collection of straw hats emphasizes the textural elements in this room and makes an attractive contrast with the straw-coloured surface of the walls. The hat-pegs are made of wood, which creates further texture in the room.*

Trimmed bedlinen

This simple technique can be used to add interest to plain white bedlinen. Contrasting, toning or matching ribbon or tape can be applied along the edge of the top sheet, and all around the pillowcases, in a single or double row. Here, yellow and green ribbons and cotton tape were used, to pick up the colours in the room. Make sure the ribbon and tape are colourfast, and are compatible in washing terms with the bedlinen. Preshrink the ribbon or tape if it is not already preshrunk.

you will need

For *trimming pillowcases*
For each pillowcase: 1.5 cm (⅝ in) wide green cotton tape • 1.5 cm (⅝ in) wide yellow cotton tape • Matching sewing threads
For *trimming sheets*
For each sheet: 3 cm (1¼ in) wide green-and-yellow ribbon • 3.5 cm (1⅜ in) wide yellow ribbon • Matching sewing threads

Pillowcases

1 Lightly mark a line about 5 cm (2 in) from all four edges of the pillowcase and pin the tape along this line. For 'housewife' pillows, pin the tape along the inner edge of the flange. Stitch along the inner edge of the tape. To mitre each corner, fold the tape back on itself and stitch diagonally between the inner and outer corners. Trim along the diagonal seamline, leaving a narrow seam allowance. Fold the tape at right angles to the previous position and pin and stitch down the next edge. Repeat for the other three edges.

2 Now take the green tape and tuck it under the outer edge of the yellow tape, again mitring the corners; pin and then stitch through both the yellow and the green tapes, using the yellow thread. Now pin and stitch the outer edge of the green tape, using the green thread. Neatly tie off the ends of the threads and trim, making sure there are no loose ends.

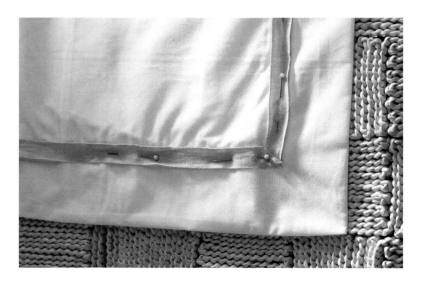

Sheet

1 Press a fold along the length of the yellow ribbon so that one side is slightly wider than the other. Wrap the folded ribbon over the edge of the sheet, with the wider side at the back. Stitch in place, being careful to keep the fold of the ribbon in contact with the edge of the sheet, and ensuring that the stitching goes through the sheet and both layers of the ribbon. Keep the ribbon and sheet taut as you stitch, to prevent puckering. Turn under the ends of the ribbon to neaten.

2 Using a pencil and ruler, mark a line about 6.5 cm (2½ in) away from the binding. Pin and stitch one edge of the yellow-and-green ribbon along this line, turning under both the ends. Now stitch the other edge of the ribbon, working in the same direction as before to keep the ribbon smooth and prevent it puckering. Neatly tie off the ends of the threads and trim, making sure there are no loose ends.

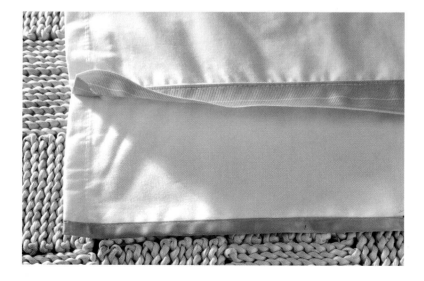

BELOW *Another texture is added in the collection of old wicker suitcases which echo the paint colours. When looking for special decorative elements to create atmosphere in a room, you do not have to be too precise or formal. A collection of cases, hatboxes or baskets piled in a corner, on top of a dresser, or hanging from simple wooden poles or pegs, looks wonderful in a country-style setting such as this.*

BELOW RIGHT *Several patterns have been mixed in this room. The quilt contains a variety of patterns, with its mixture of florals, paisley and stripes. The valance of the bed is in a pretty, traditional floral pattern in linen, in the same soft yellow as the walls. Mixing pattern in this way works well provided you ensure that cohesive elements link the schemes – for instance, you could match the size of the patterns, the colours they include or the style of pattern.*

LEFT *The attractive wooden furniture in this room is old pine, with some wicker and rush, which complements the country style. This pretty rush-seated chair goes very well with the warm yellow walls, and looks completely at home in the room. The sheer voile curtains add a white, translucent quality against the solid, plain, painted walls.*

RIGHT *The introduction of bright orange in the lampshade and the flower arrangement helps to lift the colour scheme in this bedroom. The gilding on the mirror and lamp base picks up the yellow theme but in a different texture – this time in a more elegant way – and the brilliant glossy green of the foliage in the arrangement provides a striking contrast to the orange chrysanthemums.*

CHAPTER 4

greens

Green is one of the most versatile colours in decoration, just as it provides a background role in nature – you only need to look in a garden to see how many colours green harmonizes with. Its popularity is increasing in the 1990s because it is reminiscent of the outdoors and is therefore in tune with the growing interest in environmental issues. Tranquil, relaxing and peaceful, green is, in its own way, one of the more neutral decorating colours, and as a consequence it can be mixed successfully with many others, tending to take on their character in the process.

Green is made principally from blue and yellow, so its character also varies according to how much of these two colours are used in its composition. Nature shows us the almost unlimited range of greens that are available, from the sappy greens of fresh grass shoots, new buds, unfurling leaves and young seedlings to the richer, darker greens of rose leaves, oak leaves, conifers and many other trees and plants. Perhaps as a result of green's connection with nature, it is considered a cooling, restful colour.

Paints and papers

Very dark greens, which are often called forest or bottle greens, can make good background colours for rooms in which the chief colour accent is a strong contrast, and can be used for painted walls or as the background colour in a dark patterned paper, for example. They provide a good foil for antique wooden furniture – particularly old pine – to create a strong, solid look.

Dark greens, such as forest, hunting, bottle, olive and racing greens, were much used in Victorian and Edwardian decorative schemes both in Britain and the United States, and were especially popular colour choices for hallways and studies. They were also used for painted kitchen furniture of the same period, and a particular shade of dark bluish-green, known as Paris green, has become the brand colour of Laura Ashley. A very similar green is also the brand colour of the National Trust. This shade is popular for paintwork in European countries such as France and Italy; particularly on the outsides of white houses; and for garden furniture.

For external paintwork, dark green gloss or flat oil paint is associated with the Art Nouveau movement, when it was often combined with purple in various intricately worked designs. The very dark bluish-green of the Paris Métro signs and railings is a typical example of this. A similar dark green was often used for painting front doors and, occasionally, whole houses, especially the wooden clapboard houses popular in Scandinavia and parts of the United States. It is also frequently used for outdoor garden furniture, such as ironwork benches or metal, collapsible, garden seats. Painting new fences or structures such as wooden trellises or obelisks in dark green helps them to

OPPOSITE *So predominant in nature, green, more than any other colour, links the house with the garden. In this boot room in a country house, green provides an appropriate colour scheme in a range of shades and tones, from the brilliant emerald green of the painted outhouse door to the hunting greens of the gardening boots and coats, while the vegetable print on the curtains continues the garden theme.*

blend into the background of a garden and merge with the surrounding foliage. Green is also an obvious choice for a garden room or conservatory, because it continues the verdant theme created by the plants themselves.

William Morris used green a great deal in his Arts and Crafts designs, although the shades varied considerably from rich bottle greens to pale, leafy greens. Multi-coloured chinoiserie, floral, sprigged and other informal wallpaper patterns all feature green as a co-ordinating colour, and this is often picked out for the furnishings in the rest of the room. Green is also used in many Laura Ashley wallpapers, either in its own right or as a background or secondary colour.

Fabrics

Certain themes and styles have particular associations with green. It has always formed a major colour theme in many chintz patterns, usually as the background to another colour. Many of the Arts and Crafts designs used a deep shade of green for the background colour, particularly the birds and beasts patterns made popular by William Morris at the turn of the century. Crude greens were popular in the 1950s, sharp acid green and white striped cotton was especially fashionable in the 1970s, but in the 1990s, greens have become softer and more suited to the increased interest in conservation.

Originally it was difficult to produce convincing greens in fabrics, and the colour was not successfully manufactured as a fabric dye until the 1830s. Until then, green was created for chintzes by printing blue on yellow. The yellow dyes have faded faster than the blue ones, which is why antique floral chintzes today often have blue foliage.

Deep bottle green velvet is a perennial favourite, especially when used for curtains and upholstery, while chenille is enjoying a well-deserved revival in popularity. Both have a wonderfully rich, traditional feel, with overtones of gentlemen's clubs, the green baize of snooker tables and dark green Victorian paintwork. In recent years, tartans, such as the well-known dark green and navy Black Watch pattern, have become increasingly popular, and different green-based tartans are often mixed together, employing one for a cushion cover, and another, perhaps, for the chair on which it sits.

This room demonstrates how well the Laura Ashley range of fabrics, in dark green, burgundy and taupe, work together. It also shows how much of the decorator's job of choosing harmonizing colourways is done for you when you pick fabrics, papers and paints from co-ordinated ranges. Mixing various patterns together, as here, gives an interestingly varied effect that looks natural and relaxed.

Glass and china

Wonderful, subtle shades of green are found in glassware, from the pale greenish tones of modern, inexpensive recycled glass and what is literally bottle green – the colour of dark green bottles – to the more elegant deep greens of English and Venetian glassware popular in the nineteenth century. Dark green china is also available, from sturdy, simple French café-style cups and saucers in porcelain, to the cabbage leaf and vine leaf designs that are heavily textured and glazed in various shades of green, from deep olive to emerald, so they look as if they are made from real leaves. Fine Regency china often had a border of sharp lettuce green on plain white ware, and this design is still used today. Green glazes are also very popular for rustic pottery and ironware.

Dark greens

Shades of dark green can vary quite considerably, depending on the quantities of blue, black and yellow which are mixed to make the green. Equally, dark green is known by different names in different places. In the United States it has long been called Brunswick green, whereas it is usually known in the United Kingdom as forest or bottle green. Other very similar shades of dark green include hunting green, racing green, olive

This brilliant combination of terracotta and green – colours that are diametrically opposite on the colour wheel – makes a very strong statement in this room at the Sir John Soane Museum in London. The gold relieves and brightens the colour contrast, as does the introduction of paler green, and pattern, in the carpet in the foreground.

green and Paris green. These are all classic colours which are historic in conception yet look neither dated nor dull. They translate so well to the country that they are very popular for traditional outdoor clothes, such as coats, jackets and trousers.

Olive green was particularly popular in late Victorian times, often as a background colour to more brightly printed fabrics and papers. It can appear drab when used on its own, but looks effective when lifted with lighter colours, such as yellowish- beiges and creamy whites. Bronze and gilt can also go particularly well with olive green, and furniture painted in this colour can have its handles, borders and edges picked out in gold. This is easily done using modern, cream-based gilt products.

Blue-greens

The range of blue-greens – which includes jade, teal, viridian, fir green and emerald – is large, and at the point of turquoise it becomes hard to decide whether the colour is fundamentally blue or green. It simply depends how much of each colour is used in the composition. A greenish-turquoise has become extremely popular in interior decoration for painting wooden furniture, fixtures and fittings.

Blue-green precious and semi-precious stones play a large part in the countries from which they originate. Eastern ceramics make extensive use of turquoise (the gemstone, turquoise, was first found in Turkey) and frequently combine it with russet red and a strong, cerulean blue as well as with ochre. Similar colourways are to be found in the prints of the Arts and Crafts movement, and occasionally in Art Deco designs. Jade is the sacred stone of the Orient (the translucent emerald green jade, known as 'imperial', is the most precious form) and New Zealand greenstone has great significance for Maoris.

Grey-greens

These are a particularly soft shade of green, with a considerable amount of white added to a base colour mixed from a bluish-green. They include sage, moss and misty green. Grey-green is an extremely restful colour for decoration but tends to be used only rarely as a principal colour in a scheme. It normally provides a secondary colour for brighter, but equally soft, colours such as apricot or pale powder pink. It has been used extensively in printing fabric, and is a favourite choice for Swedish painted wood and furniture. A grey-green was also much used by the Shakers and it works extremely well for very plain, painted furniture, sometimes with a contrasting border colour, such as terracotta or dusty pink.

Silver and glassware look particularly good set against a soft grey-green background, as does pewter, and a silver-greenish grey was often used as a glaze for Chinese porcelain made in the Sung dynasty (about 1000–1300 AD).

Light greens include pale moss green, apple green, aquamarine, mint, heath green and pistachio. Other light greens are eau-de-Nil, much used in the 1930s as a background colour in interior decoration, and a more astringent, sharper, green, often combined with white. Eau-de-Nil is often seen as the perfect complementary backdrop to antique furniture, particularly the brighter woods like mahogany or rosewood, and for antique paintings. It has provided the background for many English country house schemes, in which other similarly soft colours – powder blues, pale pinks and lemony yellows – are combined in floral chintzes, tapestries and faded antique Eastern carpets. Because it successfully absorbs the light, eau-de-Nil is easy to live with and easy to combine with other colours, creating a neutral, passive, reflective mood.

The fresh mossy greens are also used frequently in contemporary designs, in geometric prints such as stripes and checks, and sometimes combined in floral patterns with acid yellows and bright cobalt blues. Other light greens, such as apple green, mint and pistachio, go well with other soft ice-cream colours. When dealing with these very bright colours, you need to think carefully about the paints, papers and fabrics that you will be using and their degree of reflectivity. A matt finish is usually the most successful for this sort of colour scheme, because a reflective, shiny paint, for example, could make the colours appear to be too dominant and intrusive.

Lime green and pea green belong in this category. There is a particular shade of bright yellow-green which is very strong and makes an extremely vivid statement, so you need to plan carefully before using it. Nevertheless, it is a marvellous accent colour within a decorative scheme. It appeared in some Art Nouveau designs, was also used occasionally by the Bloomsbury group and again appeared in some of the prints of the 1950s, often combined with earth colours such as orange and brown. It can look even fresher when combined with other strong shades of blue, purple or yellow, and appears very bright when combined with white or gold.

OPPOSITE *The billiard room at Wightwick Manor in the West Midlands shows the prevailing influence of William Morris, the father of the Arts and Crafts movement. His influence extends throughout the whole house. This photograph illustrates the use of toning colours – here, a deep blue and soft sage green – which were such a trademark of the prints designed by William Morris. Stylized shapes of natural forms, such as birds, beasts and flowers, were the principal feature of most of the Arts and Crafts textiles and wallpaper designs, many of which are still in production today.*

Fresh and cheerful, light green is one of the easiest colours to live with, as this drawing room in pale moss green demonstrates. It is one of the best colours to use as a foil for the rich tones of mahogany and other fine woods. To give it life and depth, a variety of different shades of green have been incorporated in the upholstery, which gives the colour scheme harmony without appearing dull. Touches of blue and pink give vitality to this traditional English country house decorative scheme.

A Green Drawing Room

OPPOSITE *Plain, painted walls in pale moss green, with a deeper green cornice, provide a delicate foil for the distressed gold frame of the oil painting above the fireplace, which has been painted in the same shade of green. A plain background such as this plays an important part in unifying a colour scheme that employs mixed colour and pattern, and makes a link with the tonal striped wallpaper on the other walls.*

This large and spacious room has some unusual architectural features, notably the exposed stonework between the windows, the deep window recesses, the panelled walls on one side of the room and the relatively low ceiling. To counteract the effect of the latter, a light-coloured and fresh-looking decorating scheme was needed, which also increased the amount of light in the room.

The room forms part of a large country house, built several centuries ago, in a monastic settlement in East Anglia. It is important, when planning any kind of decorative scheme, to try to keep the flavour of the period in which the house was built, and also to consider its architecture. This green and white drawing room is a case in point. The ceilings of the room are very low for its large proportions, so a light and sunny scheme is appropriate to enhance the space. The simple, chintzy look, with its predominantly light green theme, is particularly suitable for the room's country setting. The panelled walls are painted to match the tonal striped wallpaper in pale moss. The windows all face on to views of grass and trees, and the interior green theme picks up this metaphor and translates it into a suitably 'gardenesque' idiom. Green is ideal for country house interiors because it combines well not only with the view through the windows but with any arrangements you make of garden flowers or foliage. Some of the most exquisite arrangements are composed entirely from foliage, and these simple green, or sometimes green and white, arrangements, loosely arranged in a large ceramic bowl or jug, are ideal for this kind of setting.

The room has been decorated in classic English country house style, using soft greens which will fade beautifully in the sun over the years. It is a room ideally suited for summer, with a door that opens straight into the garden. Pale moss, which is very similar to the colour of the lawn, has been chosen as the main wall colour to link the room with the garden beyond. An interesting mixture of large-scale floral prints has been used for the curtains and cushions to give the impression that pretty yellow, blue and pale pink cottage garden flowers are growing through green shrubbery. The antique and distressed gilded picture frames add warmth and faded elegance to the room.

Mixing patterns and colours

It is very easy, when using pattern, to become ruled by it and use too much of the same pattern throughout, which looks extremely contrived and is ultimately unrestful. You need to mix the patterns while keeping to a common theme, such as similar colours or textures. The patterns used in this room are quite varied and, as you can see, various tones and shades of the principal colour, green, have been used. You will find that if you opt for this kind of mixed pattern effect, you do not need to be too concerned about achieving an exact match of colour. You can use various shades of green – some with more yellow and some with more blue – to produce a varied effect, but you need to make sure they have roughly the same tonal value.

In this drawing room, different shades of green in similar tones have been used and blue has been introduced as a secondary colour. This makes the scheme more lively and less contrived. Some people will try to tell you that blue and green do not go together, but these colours can be used extremely successfully provided you keep the proportions in balance. Combined as they are here with white, they create an overall feeling of freshness and coolness, while spicing the mixture. It also helps if you keep the fabrics similar. For example, a blue and white toile de Jouy print in cotton looks good with a green and white cotton gingham, but if you used both a different colour and a different fabric, such as green and white silk with the blue and white toile de Jouy, the contrast would be discordant and too emphatic. By repeating a type of fabric, you create an underlying harmony which counterbalances the contrasting effect of the colour change.

Here, an apple green brushed cotton has been used on one chair and a bright emerald toile de Jouy on the other. The smaller sofa is upholstered in a simple lime green ticking and the larger one is covered in a wide stripe in moss green and white. Chambray blue has been used for a couple of the cushions and also for the checked sofa at the other end of the room. The blue forms a refreshing contrast with the green. Predominantly loose covers have been used on the furniture to continue the relaxed and informal atmosphere of the room. The white ground of the curtains keeps the scheme fresh and lively.

ABOVE *Blue and green are not commonly used together, but in this classic English country house drawing room the combination works well, creating just enough contrast to add interest, without being dominating, as a stronger contrast of, say, red and green might have been.*

OPPOSITE *Delicate arching flowerheads of geraniums adorn the deep windows in this room, the pale pink flowers echoing pink tones in the cushions on the sofas, in sympathy with the floral motif of the curtains.*

Crackle-glazing a lamp base

This is an old technique that gives a wonderful antique finish to any paintwork, so that fine hairline cracks distress the appearance of the paint, resembling an old painting. Crackle varnish comes in a kit of two bottles: the ageing varnish, which is applied first, and the crackle varnish, which is applied second. The reaction between the two causes the fine cracked lines to appear on the surface. You then need to rub a little dark pigment into the cracked surface to give it an authentically aged appearance.

you will need Sandpaper • Primer • Water-based undercoat • Base colour such as green • Crackle varnish kit (ageing varnish and crackle varnish) • Raw umber acrylic paint • Clear matt acrylic varnish

1 Lightly sand any existing paintwork, or prime the bare wood ready for painting with a suitable primer. Leave to dry, if using the primer, then apply one coat of the water-based undercoat.

2 Brush on the chosen base colour of paint (green in this case) and allow to dry. You may wish to apply more than one coat of paint in order to give a better coverage of the lamp base.

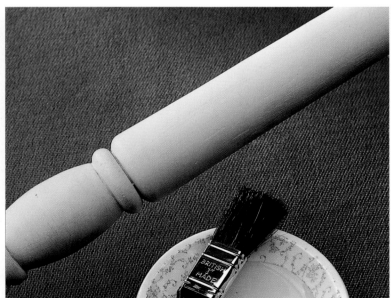

3 Apply one coat of ageing varnish and allow to dry for between 1 and 1½ hours. It should be faintly tacky to the touch, but not at all wet, and it must not dry completely. Then apply a thin coat of crackle varnish, and leave to dry overnight.

4 Rub a little raw umber (you can use raw umber acrylic paint if you wish) into the cracks, to give them an aged appearance. Leave to dry, then apply a single coat of clear matt acrylic varnish to protect the surface of the lamp base.

LEFT *In this light-filled view of the room, the subsidiary colour scheme of mid-blue is carried out in the chambray blue checked fabric of the sofa. The other colours form a contrast for the cushions. Gold-framed portraits provide additional warmth to the colour scheme, in keeping with the country house atmosphere.*

RIGHT *Simple hand-sewn triple pleated headings are a good complement to the informal style of the curtains. The use of a white ground for the fabric creates a fresh and light look which is entirely suitable for this 'gardenesque' room.*

The view of this study looks down the room, with the main window on the left-hand side. Surrounding it is a narrow green border, which helps to give definition to the window. The curtains fit neatly into the window recess, and the hand-pinched pleats are decorated with simple, large dark green chenille-covered buttons. The rich, soft colours – principally dark green, old gold and burgundy, with a few hints of navy blue and ochre – are restrained and traditional. The mahogany furniture is in keeping with the overall look, which is redolent of country gentlemen's pursuits. The walls, papered in a dark green and sand check pattern, are subtle enough to mix with other patterns in the room, such as the paisley curtains and the rich red rug.

A Green Study

This rectangular room, which measures approximately 4.9 x 3.7 metres (16 x 12 feet), can double as a guest room cum office or as a study. It has been given a deliberately masculine character, both in the choice of colours and in the style of decoration. Dark green has long been a popular colour, particularly in Victorian times when it was much in vogue for the dressing room attached to the master bedroom in large houses. It has a masculine, solid and smart appeal and, of course, it goes particularly well with the rich brown of old mahogany which was such a favourite with the Victorians.

This study has undertones of the Scottish baronial feel, partly because of the dark paisley and splashes of tartan that have been used and also because it is a formal room with dark mahogany furniture and an overall masculine quality. The atmosphere in the room is enhanced by the period of the house (parts of which were built in the fourteenth century) and the deeply recessed windows and alcoves in the room.

This close-up of the bolster and cushions on the daybed reveals a rich mixture of colours and shapes. The ends of the bolster have been covered in the same fabric as the daybed itself, while the cylindrical section of the bolster has been upholstered in green chenille. A large button, also covered in green chenille, is the finishing touch for the end of the bolster, and continues the button theme of the curtain headings. The scalloped trim, which is made from felt, on the tartan cushion picks up another theme – the scalloped baize edgings to the shelves.

Dark green is extremely restful as a decorating colour, but it usually needs a brighter contrast to give it life and warmth. In this room, sand and warm, rich burgundy have been used for this purpose, coupled with warm-coloured, antique, mahogany furniture. The walls have been papered in a simple green and sand check, and the carpet picks up the sandy colour in the walls. The fabrics follow the theme of dark green, burgundy and sand: the curtains are a beautiful, classic green and red paisley backed with a green Regency stripe fabric in dark green and burgundy on a sand background; the Queen Anne style chair is upholstered in dark green chenille with large red and green tartan patches, like the patches stitched on the elbows of a well-loved jacket; the seat of the upright chair is covered in the same tartan; and the daybed is upholstered in the green-striped fabric·used to back the curtains. You could reverse the decorative scheme and use the wide green stripe for the wallpaper, with plain curtains with a sandy background for the curtains and upholstery, and the paisley fabric on the chair, but you would need to add more red as a contrast because the overall effect would be darker and heavier.

The fabrics gain much of their richness not only from the colour but also from the rich texture of the weave. It is appropriate that these deep colours are used on a sand background because if they were set against white the contrast would be too jarring.

One of the unusual and most interesting features of this room is the way that different fabrics and patterns have been used to complement each other. The rich, deep green paisley curtains have been lined, luxuriously, with a patterned fabric that picks up the same colours in its simple, bold stripe. This adds elegance to the room. These dark, traditional colours form a wonderful backdrop for the collection of old books, school and college memorabilia and sporting trophies which adorn the room.

Here you can see how two contrasting fabrics have been combined for the curtains, with the dark green, burgundy and sand stripes creating the lining for the main fabric, a traditional rich paisley in the same colours.

Double-sided screen

Screens can be made from a variety of materials; this one is made from chipboard in two hinged panels. One side is decorated with photocopies of antique maps; old newspaper cuttings, left-over pieces of expensive wallpaper or family memorabilia, such as letters, certificates or school reports, would be equally suitable. The weight of the papers should be roughly similar and ideally they should not be too thick. The other side of the screen is a simple noticeboard, made of baize criss-crossed with ribbon. The baize is secured with staples and the edges covered with strips of upholstery studs; these resemble single upholstery nailing, but are much less time-consuming to use because the nails are inserted at intervals, rather than one by one.

you will need Proprietary primer • Maps, old newspaper cuttings, letters, etc. • Wallpaper paste • Sponge • Damp cloth • Clear acrylic varnish • Raw umber acrylic paint • Chipboard or hardboard screen • Green baize • Narrow ribbon • Staple gun • Strips of upholstery studs, and also single upholstery studs • Tailor's chalk

1 If you are making a screen yourself, prime it first with a proprietary primer. Apply wallpaper paste to the screen and the backs of the maps or paper. Position on the screen, carefully brushing out from the centre. Check the edges are well glued, and smooth flat with a sponge. Wipe off surplus paste with a damp cloth. Leave to dry, then brush on a thin coat of varnish. Leave to dry. Mix a tiny amount of raw umber acrylic paint with a little varnish to make it runny, then add it to the varnish in small drops. Apply the varnish, leave to dry.

2 Measure the screen and mark out these measurements on the baize, allowing enough extra all round to cover the edges of the screen as well. Cut the baize slightly larger all round than you need. Stretch it over the screen and staple it in position at the sides with a staple gun, making sure that there are no creases or folds in the baize.

3 To finish off the sides of the screen in a decorative way, nail strips of upholstery studding down all the four sides, to cover the edges of the baize and the staples.

4 Measure a trellis grid for the ribbon on the screen with tailor's chalk. This particular trellis pattern has a 25 cm (10 in) distance between the ribbons. Fix the ribbon to the screen over the chalked lines with a single upholstery pin at each end, and at each intersection point of the ribbons.

A special finishing touch, which picks up the baize theme from the screen, is the scalloped decorative edging, cut from strips of green baize, for the bookcase shelves. To make this, you must first measure the length of the shelves. Then measure their depth and double it. Cut out a strip of baize to these dimensions for each shelf that will be edged. Of course, if the size of the shelves varies, you will have to measure each one separately. Mark the scallops along the long edge of the baize using an appropriate circle-shaped guide, such as the base of an egg cup, for example, in ballpoint pen, felt tip or tailor's chalk. Cut out the scalloped border with a pair of sharp scissors. Fix the edging to each shelf with a row of brass studs.

One of the more novel uses of fabric in this room is the way that the arms of the Queen Anne style chair have been patched with a contrasting tartan fabric, in much the same way that the elbows of a favourite tweed jacket can be reinforced with leather when they start to show signs of wear. Although practical in inspiration, the patches can be purely decorative and will give a novel edge to a simple piece of upholstered furniture. Choose a fabric which co-ordinates with the main upholstery in colour and pattern, but look for similar fabric weights and weaves – for example, do not mix cotton with silk. You could patch plain cotton rep with gingham, or a figured damask with a floral pattern in heavy linen union. With this chair, the colourways have a similar density of tone. This means that, although the patches are visible, they do not stand out too prominently which they would, for example, if the tartan pattern contained white or an equally pale colour.

Decorative scalloped edging

The armchair patches

LEFT *The shelves on which the books are arranged have been edged with decorative baize scallops. This is a useful device for covering less than wonderful wooden shelves or, indeed, white melamine shelves that are out of sympathy with the rest of a decorative scheme.*

RIGHT *This detail reveals the decorative blanket stitch around the edge of the patches on the armchair. This is for decoration only – any raw edges are best hemmed with zigzag stitch first to stop them fraying. You can stick the patches to fixed upholstery with double-sided adhesive tape, but they are easily stitched to loose covers. A contrasting tartan cushion picks out the tartan patches.*

There are several different curtain treatments in this room, partly because the room's three window recesses all vary. When planning curtain designs, it is important to take account of the scale and proportion of the windows and surrounding walls. In some cases, it is not possible to run a pelmet across the window because it would take away too much light, or look ungainly. When there is little space, you are probably best advised to choose an attractive curtain heading with a neat, simple finish, as has been done here on one set of curtains with the hand-sewn pinch pleats, finished with buttons.

When it is possible to include a pelmet, keep it in sympathy with the shape of the window and the overall feel of the room. Make sure that the weight and shape of the pelmet suits the drop of the curtains and also their thickness. A quilted and padded self-fabric pelmet, edged with the lining fabric, has been used here to neaten and smarten the smallest window.

Curtain treatments

OPPOSITE *This view shows the very different styles of window in the room. Although this is relatively rare in modern houses, it is a frequent feature of old houses, or where a couple of rooms have been knocked together. At the larger window, the curtains have been fitted neatly into the recess. At the smaller window, they hang outside it, topped with a self-fabric pelmet.*

ABOVE RIGHT *The heavily padded and quilted self-fabric pelmet runs across the top of the smaller window. A subtle but effective detail is the rolled and padded edging, used like a braid, in the wide green stripe of the lining fabric. This picks up and emphasizes the off-white in the paisley pattern.*

RIGHT *These paisley curtains have been given deep, hand-sewn pinch-pleat headings, each pleat adorned with a large button covered in dark green chenille for emphasis. Note how the buttons provide a valuable colour link with the dark green border detail surrounding the window recess. Small touches such as these make all the difference in a decorative scheme by pulling it together and ensuring that the overall effect is unified. This is particularly important when several colours are used in one room, as they are here.*

CHAPTER 5

blues

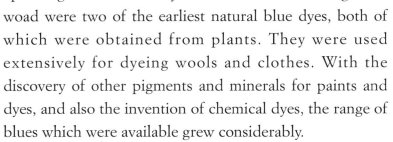

Blue is one of the most relaxing colours of all. It is generally associated with tranquillity and harmony, perhaps in part from its connotations with the sky and water, and colour therapists advise us to wear blue when we are feeling under stress. The colour range is enormous: the deepest midnight blues and ultramarines; regal blues such as navy, Prussian and Windsor; denim; delphinium; deep sapphire; bright Mediterranean blue, cobalt and cerulean; sky blue; cornflower blue; china blue; duck egg blue; chambray; ice blue; Wedgwood blue; forget-me-not blue; smoke; azure; Adam blue; and many others, including blues that are nearly purple (with plenty of red in their composition) and blues that are almost turquoise (with masses of green). For our purposes in this book, the colour includes the more bluish-mauves as well, such as lavender and amethyst. It is interesting to note how many of the blues we know are named after flowers. The pigment, blue, derives from three main colours – cobalt blue, ultramarine and Prussian blue – all of which are fairly warm blues with a certain amount of red in them.

Among the first blue pigments were lapis lazuli, indigo and woad. Lapis lazuli was very expensive, so was only used in paintings for the wealthy or for the Church. Indigo and woad were two of the earliest natural blue dyes, both of which were obtained from plants. They were used extensively for dyeing wools and clothes. With the discovery of other pigments and minerals for paints and dyes, and also the invention of chemical dyes, the range of blues which were available grew considerably.

The vibrancy of blue shows up wonderfully in paintings, and many artists have used it to great effect. Lapis lazuli was used a great deal in the religious paintings and frescoes of the Renaissance, while more modern works of art use other shades of blue – Turner's seascapes were full of cold blues; Matisse's paintings used vivid, hot blues; Monet's series of waterlily paintings featured sea blues and misty lavenders; Dufy's watercolours of the French Riviera combined cool and warm blues; and Picasso is renowned for his 'blue period'. Blues used in the manufacture of porcelain, such as Wedgwood blue and the blues of willow pattern china, have also considerably increased the popularity of the colour.

Like all colours, blue varies a great deal, not only

Blue and white is one of the most popular colour combinations. This collection of cushions makes use of rich mid-blue and white in a range of patterns as a contrast, with stripes and florals, checks and novelty prints mixed and matched in a variety of styles and shapes. The main cushion cover has been given a buttoned-on front panel – a quirky way to update a plain cushion.

depending on the intensity of the hue and the tone or shade (see page 14), but by virtue of the colour or colours you choose to combine with it. A combination of different tones of blue can look very effective, perhaps with small splashes of white, yellow or another pale colour to break it up. Alternatively, you could introduce a stronger, contrasting colour that brings the blues alive. Colours tend to take on a different feel according to the other colours they are mixed with: if you put blue and red together, the blue will automatically look warmer; if you combine it with green, it will look cooler. In this way, you can change the effect of the particular blue you are using through careful choice of other colours, and you should be aware of this when deciding which colour to put with blue. This is also an important rule to remember when choosing blue for a room that receives little light – unless you are careful about the particular shades of blue that you choose (using one that is very warm), and the other colours in the scheme, the finished effect can be very cold and unwelcoming.

Blue can be used for many different looks in the house, from the simple, rustic appeal of Mediterranean blue and white to much richer, deeper blues, combined with yellows, golds or reds in an exotic, sophisticated combination. Particular shades of blue have special geographical or historical connotations – the Mediterranean blue mentioned above is a very clear, bright, pure blue which can stand up to the area's strong sunshine, while paler blues would look bleached out; a paler, cool grey-blue is frequently used in Scandinavian interiors; and Persian mosaics feature strong royal blues. A wonderfully rich turquoise blue is associated with Sèvres porcelain.

Fabrics

Blue is one of the colours used most often in fabrics, and frequently in geometric patterns – very successfully when combined with white or off-white in plain ginghams and broad stripes in various weights of cotton. Indigo is also one of the principal colours in the figurative toile de Jouy fabrics.

Deep navy blues work particularly well for velvets, chenilles and damasks, as well as toiles, tickings and ginghams. They can all look good when trimmed and edged in a contrasting, brighter colour, such as emerald green or rich, ruby red. Many shades of blue create a fresh, sprigged look for country-style cottons, often on a white ground, and with the addition of other mid-tone colours, particularly yellows and greens, for a clear, spring-like effect. Provençal fabrics feature a lovely, warm blue, often combined with yellow and red. Blue Laura Ashley fabrics in such shades as sapphire, smoke, emperor blue, china blue, chambray and classic navy are among the most popular in the entire range. They all look very fresh when combined with white, very pretty when used with pale pink, bright when combined with hot pink and lime green, and very rich when accompanied by golds, ochres and burgundies.

Because of its colour associations with water and the sea, patterns using blue sometimes have nautical or seaside overtones in novelty prints for quirky decorating – shells and boats are particularly popular. For the same reason, blue is often chosen for bathrooms, where a combination of blue and white is particularly successful because it looks so clean. The mid-blues that have quite a lot of red in their composition are much warmer and therefore much easier to use successfully.

Furniture   Blue is particularly effective when used for painted wooden furniture. In France, for example, it is almost obligatory to paint your shutters that wonderful pale blue reminiscent of faded denims. Blue – in particular, a fairly deep, pure blue – can be used successfully to antique and distress wooden furniture, which makes it an ideal colour choice for an old pine dresser or simple kitchen cabinet. Much paler shades of a grey-blue have also been used a great deal in Scandinavian painted furniture, often with soft creams and a pale greyish-white. Smoky blue is particularly suitable for creating a Shaker look for paintwork and furniture. Try using it with a pale sandy yellow, rather than the sharper contrast of white. You could decorate a cottage kitchen in these colours, with a simple blue and white checked fabric and a dresser in distressed smoky blue.

Deep warm blues   The deeper, warmer shades of blue, such as navy, Prussian, Windsor, denim and emperor blue, are generally based on two particular colours – ultramarine for paint dyes and indigo for textile dyes. These deep blues can be used over quite large areas: for wallpapers, perhaps, that combine the blue with a lighter colour such as sand; or for fabrics, as upholstery on chairs and sofas or as curtains.

You need to find a complementary colour to offset large areas of quite strong colour. White is normally the chosen contrast, although such colours as yellow and plaster pink work equally well, according to the effect you wish to achieve. Navy, burgundy and sand is another good combination. The colour you choose will depend on the atmosphere you want to create, and on the amount of light the room receives. White will give a crisp, clean contrast, but yellow or orange may give a more unusual, contemporary effect and will really bring out the richness of the blue to make the room glow. For a very rich, smart and elegant room, you could use navy, burgundy and gold.

Small areas, such as cloakrooms and tiny kitchens, can be enhanced by painting or papering the walls in deep, rich blues – they go extremely well with warm mahogany

Simple, brilliant blue shutters against a plain white wall make a wonderfully strong colour statement. This particular shade of blue – pure and warm – is one of the easiest to live with and combines particularly well with white. It succeeds in looking both modern and bright, but with a strong feeling of nature, no doubt from its connotations with the sea and the sky.

furniture, and will provide an excellent foil for blue and white china or other bright decorative elements, such as storage jars or cooking utensils in the kitchen. Try contrasting these blues with deep, rich reds, dark greens and golds for the look of Victorian polychromy – the starting point could perhaps be a piece of maiolica ware in these three colours.

Mid-blues

If you opt for the richness of the Empire look, you can cover the walls in a mid-blue such as cobalt, cerulean or deep sapphire. Self-toned stripes or a self-patterned damask-type paper provides a good background for showing off collections of paintings, prints or china. Window treatments can be equally opulent in this colour scheme, with swags if the windows are grand enough to take them, and perhaps fringes or tassels on the pelmets or as borders to the curtains. A similar shade of blue can also be used for a simple, country cottage scheme, using plain cotton fabrics, rag rugs and colourwashed walls. A bedroom in this vein might well have plain white linen on the bed itself, and white muslin bed drapes, or could look very contemporary with a wrought-iron bedstead.

OPPOSITE *Sapphire blue is a particularly gentle colour. It is part of the many different patterns used for the fabrics here, all of which are Laura Ashley designs. This room demonstrates how to use pattern to create visual interest when the colour palette is strictly limited.*

The scheme can equally be inverted, painting the walls white or off-white, and picking out the woodwork – skirting, dado or picture rail and doorways – in the deepish mid-blue, with the upholstery and patterned fabrics in different tones of blue, mixed with one other colour – brick red, perhaps, or peacock blue.

You can sometimes play successfully with different shades of blue, contrasting peacock blues (which contain a lot of green) with much warmer chalky blues, lavenders with turquoise, and so on. This could work successfully in a predominantly blue kitchen where simple kitchen furniture is painted in a range of blues, the room dominated perhaps by a lustrous, deep blue Aga. When playing with different shades of blue in this way, eschew white as a contrast and pick a complementary colour with the same tonal values – a mid-green, perhaps, or a warm yellow.

Lighter, warm blues

Often associated with house-painting at the seaside, these blues – wonderful pure, powdery cobalt mixed with white in such shades as sapphire, deep powder blue and azure – can form the core of many decorative schemes in a range of styles, from Mediterranean to American colonial. Much depends on how and where these blues are used, whether for sophisticated self-striped wallpaper or for roughly-painted stone. They make an excellent backdrop for the walls, doorways and windows of country cottages, especially when combined with another colour of matching intensity – perhaps a green or a yellow – for other items of furniture, whether they have been upholstered or painted.

Blue-greens   Cool, blue-greens, such as duck egg blue, aquamarine, turquoise blue, Williamsburg blue, Wedgwood and Adam blue, need to be handled with care. They can look very cold and uninviting unless used in conjunction with warm-looking materials, such as wood, or combined with a warmer colour, such as apricot or soft russet. Cream or off-white makes a less clinical contrast than pure white, and blue-green fabrics can sometimes look warmer in matt, woven forms rather than in shiny silks or chintzes. Blue-greens are often chosen for bathrooms, perhaps on the basis that, as they are reminiscent of the colour of the sea they are the most appropriate choice. Painting in an old-fashioned matt paint would help to warm the colour by giving it depth, as would combining it with warm-coloured woods such as pine or oak.

Blue and yellow   This is a particularly attractive combination, because the colours are complementary in the colour spectrum. As a result, the warmth of the yellow compensates for any inherent coldness in the blue tones, and gives them the life and zest they need. The combination of blue and yellow conjures up visions of summer wheatfields set against a deep blue sky. Blue and yellow has become a very contemporary colour scheme. It was used a great deal in the 1980s when yellow became a popular colour, and was partly inspired by the work of such artists as Van Gogh, who used these colours in a vibrant way.

Balancing the intensity of the blue and yellow hues is an important factor in the success of this kind of scheme – for it to work best, the intensity of each colour must be of equal saturation, as in bright cerulean blue and sunshine yellow, or pale duck egg blue and pale primrose. This colour scheme also works well when one colour is used as an accent. For example, you could choose deep sunflower or cowslip for the walls, with accents of delphinium blue as the cushions, curtain edgings and lampshades. When decorating a room in fairly equal amounts of two colours, such as blue and yellow, the aim is to ensure that the areas of colour are equally balanced, so neither colour predominates. Beware of arranging the colours too symmetrically, however, or they will look contrived. If you pick yellow for the walls, then use mostly blue for the furnishings, and use the yellow again for small touches such as cushions, chair seats and curtain ties.

Blue and green   An old saying runs 'blue and green should never be seen'. Yet we do see the combination often enough in nature, and indeed blue flowers such as cornflowers and delphiniums are among the most popular of all. Gardens can be the inspiration for peaceful and relaxing country cottage colour schemes of blue and green, with touches of white or cream, particularly when combined in simple, floral patterns. For this kind of look, you could use mid-blues and mid-greens. The blues have a high proportion of green in them and the greens contain a strong element of blue, thereby creating a balanced match. Looking through gardening magazines and books will help you to find good matches of blue and green if you are in need of inspiration.

Blue and green are also used in Indian cottons and Provençal fabrics, with their evocations of wide landscapes, grassy swards and relaxed informality. When used in conjunction with large expanses of white or off-white for the walls or floors, for example, the decor is given a fresh, almost seaside look. Another version of the blue/green colour combination is dark blue with vivid emerald green, especially when other colours are included in the scheme to add more life – a golden yellow, perhaps, or a strong Indian red. This combination can be used to create a rich, opulent, Empire or colonial look, with lustrous fabrics, embossed wallpapers, beautiful antique textiles and gilded or colonial furniture.

Blue and pink was especially popular in the eighteenth century, when a particular shade of powder blue was often combined with a soft pastel pink, frequently with gilded decoration. The style, known as rococo, was all the rage throughout Europe, and the combination of blue and pink was one of its hallmarks. The colour scheme was also used on the Sèvres porcelain of the period, although the Sèvres blue was far more turquoise than pure blue. The circular closet at Syon House, in London, was decorated by John Fowler (of Colefax and Fowler) in precisely these sugar-candy pink and blue shades, with the delicate detailing picked out in gold leaf. Another, less formal, scheme by John Fowler for a country bedroom combined blue and pink – the walls were given pale pink stripes, and the pelmet of the pink silk curtains was edged with deep violet blue braid and tassels. The bedroom furniture was mahogany, and some of the chairs had blue and pink tapestry seats.

This softly contrasting combination of muted blues and pinks works particularly well for bedrooms, especially when teamed with slightly faded-looking floral patterns and delicately painted furniture. It goes well, too, with stencilling and stamping, and a smoky blue-grey works well with a soft, muted pink. In deeper tone, raspberry pink and a much deeper mid-blue containing a little red,

Blue and pink

In this pretty country room, the chambray blue walls form the perfect backdrop to the blue and pink curtains edged in blue.

such as a kingfisher blue, can be made to work well together, provided you use similar colour saturations of each tone. The warmth of the raspberry compensates for any coldness in the blue, and could work well in a shady room, for example, where blue and white, the more classic combination, might look too cool and unfriendly. Raspberry and mid-blue combines well with deeper toned woods, such as rosewood and mahogany, in a more traditional look, with fabrics in thick damasks, chenilles or velvets, and using more formal prints rather than pretty florals.

Blue and terracotta

Relatively recently, a very rich, warm, colour combination of a slate-grey blue and brick red or terracotta became fashionable. It takes its emblem from the earth pigments of Mexico, in particular, and translates well into a simple design style, using rustic furniture, strong outlines and relatively little pattern. With this type of colour scheme, it pays to concentrate on surface and texture, as do the original colours in their native environment – roughly-painted plaster and brick, and weathered and distressed furniture. This colour scheme might work for a simple, unfitted kitchen or a hallway, combined with a natural terracotta floor. It might also work well in an informal bathroom.

Blue and white

OPPOSITE *Blue and white is one of the most popular colour combinations of all. Here, a soft deep blue has been used for the wall of a clapboard house in America, while the ornate mouldings of the woodwork have been picked out in white. Whether used for collections of china or in textiles, this deep blue, combined with white, is one of the most enduring colour schemes because it is traditional yet looks fresh.*

The three colours from which blue pigment is derived – cobalt blue, ultramarine and Prussian blue – combine extremely well with white, either as a contrast or to make a paler hue of the particular blue that is being used. This classic decorating combination of blue and white undoubtedly stemmed from its success in the decorative art of ceramics. Blue was one of the purest colours available as a glaze and therefore became popular all over the world.

In fact, the combination of blue and white is one of the most popular of all time, with some very famous associations. The inspiration for a lot of blue and white china is Chinese, dating from before the fifteenth century, and including such famous dynasties as Ming (which means 'luminous' in Mandarin), featuring representational images in deep blue on a white ground. A variety of patterns and motifs was used, ranging from botanical designs such as acanthus leaves to animals and birds, all of which were symbolic. Islamic countries, also began to produce their own designs of blue and white china, mostly in geometric designs on ceramic tiles. From here, the practice spread to Italy, where it featured in maiolica ware, then the Netherlands, where it is known as Delft china, and finally to Britain.

When blue and white china arrived in Britain in the late eighteenth century, famous porcelain houses such as Worcester first made delicate blue and white tea ware in imitation of Chinese porcelain, complete with Oriental scenes and figures. In the following century, willow pattern china – a European design inspired by Chinese porcelain – was developed by such factories as Spode and became immensely popular. There was a profusion of blue and white transfer-printed china, including Spode's highly decorated Blue Italian design which depicts a classical Italian lake scene. Indian designs were also popular, inspired by engravings and delicate botanical prints. The Wedgwood factory produced their own blue and white trademark, known as jasperware, which featured classical figures in white cameo relief on unglazed blue or other coloured backgrounds. This followed the neo-Classical taste of the time, and was so sophisticated that rooms are still decorated in what has become known as Wedgwood blue, with paintwork, ceiling and cornices picked out in white in the style of Robert Adam. Later came 'flow blue', which has a darker blue glaze which literally flows over the outline of the transfer. It is very popular in the United States, as is the contemporary blue and white mottled enamel ware known as spatterware. Another rustic style of pottery is Cornish breakfast ware, which features simple, wide blue and white stripes.

When mixing blue and white, there are just as many designs and variations as in any other combination with blue, but certain themes are perennially popular. Stripes work particularly well in blue and white, whether in broad, even bands of chalky blue and white in such fabrics as calico, sailcloth or canvas, or as dark navy and white ticking. Checks, such as ginghams, are also very attractive. The effect is clear, clean, modern and simple, and combines well with other more elaborate representational patterns, such as blue and white toile de Jouy fabrics, and large blue and white cabbage roses in chintz or linen union. Fabrics and wallpapers featuring multi-coloured chinoiserie and botanical prints are often re-coloured and printed in a purely blue and white colourway. The original colours are replaced by varying shades of blue on a white ground to give a crisp and elegant design.

Blue and white tiles

The well-known landscape and seascape designs in blue on a white ground are immediately recognizable as Delft – the term used to describe tin-glazed ceramic tiles manufactured in the Netherlands in the seventeenth century. The tin glaze that made the distinctive Delft tiles – and their forerunners, sixteenth-century European maiolica ware – comes from adding tin oxide to the lead glazes that are generally used. This transforms the ordinary orange clay into the delicate creamy white ground that was used by the painters as a canvas for their brilliantly coloured designs and which is such a hallmark of tin glaze ware. The deep, rich blue so characteristic of Delftware was formed by adding cobalt to the lead glaze. This technique was first used in southern Spain in the eleventh century, and a range of blue and white patterns is to be found in many countries around the shores of the Mediterranean.

One of the influences for Delft designs came from the Dutch East India Company's supply of Chinese porcelain, which was being imported from the Far East, and the resulting desire to create a cheaper, home-produced version. Civil war in China in the 1650s provided the trigger for massively increased production of blue and white tiles in Holland. The industry centred on the town of Delft, which is how the china came to be so named. The range of subjects used for the tiles extended into all sorts of naturalized objects, including flowers, animals and scenes from everyday life including boats and canals. The tiles were extremely popular outside as well as inside the Netherlands, and a thriving export industry developed. They are still popular today.

As the tiles were delicate, they were better suited for covering walls rather than floors. They were used in a whole range of applications, often as skirting boards and to line the large, recessed fireplaces that were a feature of Dutch interiors of the time. Even whole walls were lined with Delft tiles, with the deeper blue tones accentuated by the paintwork on the architraves, window frames and fire surrounds. The patterns and colourways so popular in tiles can be translated successfully into fabrics, either using patchwork or appliqué techniques, or can be stencilled on to painted surfaces, such as an occasional table or cupboard door.

OPPOSITE *Monet's house in France demonstrates a rich and exciting use of colour, as befits one of the major colourists in the French Impressionist movement. Here, in this photograph of a corner of the kitchen, the warm tones of the copper cooking utensils make a rich contrast of texture and colour against the cool blue and white tiles, and the blue and white kitchen cupboards.*

The rich, chestnut-coloured floorboards in this light, cheerful family room provide a welcome warm contrast to the cool blue and white theme which forms the major decorating concept, based on the collection of blue and white china displayed on the dresser. The theme is taken up in the various fabrics, from the simple gingham chair seats, through to the antique toile de Jouy dress curtains.

upholstery-weight gingham, neatly self-piped with a double edge. A long settle on the other side of the table has been given a rectangular squab cushion, which is tied to the wooden seat at the corners with simple self-ties. Over the sink, the shelves have been dragged in light blue over a white-painted background.

Appliqué tablecloth

To make a tablecloth similar to the one shown, you will need a plain white damask cloth, together with some scraps of blue and white cotton fabric, in a variety of designs. You will also need a fixing fabric, such as Bondaweb, which can be obtained from any good haberdashery department. The method shown is quick and easy but would not stand up to repeated washing, as the cut fabric edges would fray. (For a more permanent design for everyday use, you would need to finish the edges of the appliqué motifs, either by zigzag stitching after applying them to the cloth or by turning under a seam allowance – which is added to the motifs prior to cutting them out – and slip-stitching them on to the tablecloth by hand instead of using Bondaweb.) The steps below are for fixing the motifs to the cloth, without finishing the edges.

you will need

White damask tablecloth • Scraps of several blue and white patterned fabrics • Small piece of plain fabric, for backing (not visible) • Bondaweb • Blue embroidery thread • Blue sewing thread

1 Draw a teapot on a piece of paper and cut it out. Place the template on a piece of plain fabric and cut around it. Iron a piece of Bondaweb to the front of the fabric teapot, having first covered the ironing board with a piece of old fabric or paper.

2 Peel off the paper covering the Bondaweb. From the patterned fabrics, cut out shapes to fit the teapot – the body of the pot, spout, handle, base, lid, etc. – and arrange them on the Bondaweb-covered teapot like a collage. Iron the fabric shapes in position.

3 Iron another piece of Bondaweb on to the reverse side of the teapot. Iron this motif on to the centre of the tablecloth. Using blue sewing thread, embellish the teapot with handstitches around the edges of the fabric shapes.

4 Appliqué cups-and-saucers and spoons to the tablecloth in the same way. Using blue embroidery thread, work running stitches to represent steam above each teacup, then embroider a scallop pattern around the edge of the tablecloth with running stitch.

Stencilling a design

To create a stencilled design from one of your own sources, you will need to be able to cut out a stencil yourself. This is normally done on oiled card (which is available from any art supplier), and you will also need a scalpel blade or other sharp craft knife. Lay a piece of tracing paper over the design and trace over the outline with a soft 2B pencil. Then turn the traced design over, place it on the stencil card and rub over the back with a hard object so that the image is transferred on to the stencil card. Place the stencil card on a cutting board and cut around the edge of the pencil line very carefully, using a scalpel blade or another extremely sharp knife.

To use the stencil, you will need to use masking tape to tape it to the object being painted, because this tape peels off without marking the paintwork. If you are creating a border or repeating pattern, you will need to make registration marks (small holes) in the edges of the stencil card so you can line up the pattern accurately as you move along the surface which is being painted.

To paint the stencil, you will need either purpose-bought stencil paints or ordinary emulsion. The paint must be fairly thick and not runny, otherwise it will run under the edges of the stencil and ruin the image. You will also need a short, stubby bristled brush called a stencilling brush. Mix or turn the paint into a tray and dip the stencil brush into the paint. Dab any surplus paint off the brush on to a piece of spare card, until the amount of paint on the card no longer looks thick and blobby. Then, using an up and down motion of the wrist, pounce the paint through the holes in the stencil design. You may prefer to practise first on a spare piece of card if you are not used to stencilling, or want to check that you like the stencil you have made.

The stencilled design in this room was then picked out further with simple brush strokes and the border was painted in a deeper shade of blue for added definition.

BELOW A plain white damask tablecloth has been given a new lease of life with appliqué motifs in blue and white. The blue and white china theme that inspired this cloth came from the owner's collection of china shown on the dresser on page 161. You can create as many or as few appliqué motifs as you wish, which are either machine or handstitched.

RIGHT A small stencilled border has been added to the front edge of the mantelpiece, the inspiration for it taken from the design on a china plate. Ornaments of all descriptions provide valuable source material for decorating concepts, whether in terms of colour mixing or pattern making. The informal arrangement of white cottage garden flowers suits the relaxed mood of the room.

LEFT *A neat frame of a blue and white ticking pelmet and side covers has been given to the white dresser displaying the blue and white china. Frequently seen in Dutch houses, these simple fabric decorations for shelves and mantelpieces make an attractive addition to what is otherwise a simple piece of furniture.*

BOTTOM LEFT *Mixing pattern can have an exciting and uplifting effect on any decorative scheme. Here, a willow pattern design, echoing that of the china elsewhere in the room, has been employed for a frilled cushion on this country-style wicker chair, upholstered and buttoned in blue and white check.*

RIGHT *The eclectic blue and white china collection, displayed to good effect against the plain white backdrop of the dresser, provides the inspiration for the mixture of colours and patterns in this room.*

This blue and yellow bedroom
has a fresh, country appeal that
derives in part from the colour
combination and in part from
the use of simple cotton fabrics.
While the chambray blue
colourwashed walls provide the
basis of the scheme, the touches
of cowslip yellow – to frame the
walls at ceiling and skirting
board height, in the bedspread
and the reverse and ties of the
curtains – give it life and a
contemporary twist.

A Blue & Yellow Bedroom

In this room, chambray blue is combined with bright cowslip yellow. Each colour has the same degree of saturation, which means that the two colours balance each other. This is an important aspect in the successful combining of strong, bright colours. The addition of yellow helps to give life and colour to the blue.. On its own, or combined with a less forthright colour, the blue would tend to recede, even though it is quite strong. The blue here contains quite a lot of red, which pushes it towards the warmer end of the blue spectrum. The yellow also has red in its composition, which gives the two colours a unity and harmony they might otherwise lack. The same principle could be used with a more greeny-yellow and a more yellowy-blue. The addition of small touches of pink and purplish-blue also emphasize the warm tones inherent in this colour mixture. This makes it cheerful, friendly and welcoming, and suits the simple charm of the furnishings and fabrics extremely well.

This room is fresh, simple, unpretentious and youthful in appearance. The Provençal feeling of the room is created by the patchwork quilt and the use of gingham, as well as the choice of colours. The French theme is continued in the simple cotton used for the curtains – a bright chambray trefoil pattern has been used for the outside of the curtains which are lined with the same trefoil pattern in cowslip, which is also used to make the curtain heading. Equally French is the subtle addition of hot pink picked out in the flowers, the pattern on the quilt and some of the plates. A secondary theme is blue and white, used for the scalloped skirt for the dressing table, the scalloped trim over the mantelpiece, the valance of the bed and the blue and white china.

This is a country room, yet it is also sophisticated in the way it combines colour and pattern and also in its details – a yellow border runs around the skirting board and another acts as a cornice; scallops appear on the mantelpiece, bed valance and dressing table; and a pelmet board sits over the windows on which blue and white plates are displayed. All these decorative effects create a charming and timeless bedroom.

Colourwashed wallpaper provides a watery textured background, contrasted with brilliant white paintwork and the bright cowslip yellow borders at both ceiling and skirting height. These borders are an essential ingredient of the room because they consolidate the yellow theme without being overwhelming. Such borders are easy to paint: all you need do is fix masking tape to the wall, to give you a straight line to paint along and to mask off the remaining paintwork. When the paint is completely dry, you peel off the tape to reveal the coloured border. If you wish, you can paint the contrasting strip around the edge of each wall, to create a panelled effect. An alternative to painting the borders would be to use a wallpaper border which you might find easier to manage.

OPPOSITE *A rich tapestry of blue and yellow is created by the stripes of the cotton dhurrie on the floor, the scalloped chambray blue bed valance and the deep yellow border of the quilt, set against the matching blue fabric of the dressing table skirt and the curtains beyond.*

Scalloped gingham trim

This fresh gingham mantelpiece trim with its piped, scalloped edge makes a charming background for ornaments in the same colours. You can adjust the size of the scallops to the dimensions of your mantelpiece. To do this, you simply decide the approximate size of your scallops, and divide this into the length around the mantelpiece (i.e. the front plus both ends) to get the number of scallops. If it is not a whole number, round the number up or down and divide it back into the length measurement. That figure is the exact width of each scallop, measured at the widest point.

you will need Fabric such as checked gingham • Pair of compasses • Piping cord • Sewing thread • Fabric marker

1 Cut two strips of fabric to the total length around the mantelpiece (front plus both ends) plus 2 cm (¾ in), and to a width of half the width of each scallop plus 2.5 cm (1 in). Make a template – use a pair of compasses to draw the correct number of scallops as a line of semi-circles to the size you calculated. With a fabric marker, draw round the template on to the wrong side of one of the fabric strips, leaving 1 cm (⅜ in) between the scalloped edge of the template and the edge of the strip. With right sides together and raw edges even, stitch the two strips together along the scalloped line. Trim 1 cm (⅜ in) outside the stitched line, clip the curves, turn right sides out and press.

2 Cut 5 cm (2 in) wide bias strips and join them with diagonal seams, until you have a strip the length of the scalloped piece. Wrap the bias strip around piping cord and stitch close to the cord, using the piping or zip foot on your machine. Cut a strip of fabric to the actual length of the mantelpiece plus 3 cm (1¼ in), by twice the depth of the mantelpiece plus 3 cm (1¼ in). Cut the strip so the patterns match when the scalloped strip is attached. Right sides together, pin the piping along one long edge and across half of each end of the strip, positioning it just inside the seamline, with the stitching 1.5 cm (⅝ in) from the edge. Clip into the seam allowance at the corners. Stitch.

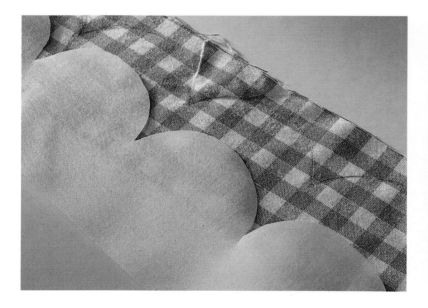 

3 Place the scalloped piece on top of the piping, also facing inwards, matching the patterns. Pin and baste. Fold in half lengthwise, right sides together, and stitch along the seamline, 1.5 cm (⅝ in) from the edge, across both ends and along the long edge, leaving an opening.

4 Turn the mantelpiece trimming right sides out, through the small opening which you have left, and press. Slip-stitch the opening, using a coloured thread that matches the colour of the mantelpiece trim, to close it. Fasten off the ends of the thread neatly.

These chambray curtains hang from a brass curtain pole. Their contrasting ties, in a cowslip colourway of the same fabric, echo the narrow painted border of cowslip yellow at ceiling height. The old pelmet board serves as a display shelf for a collection of antique plates.

A simple vase of cottage garden flowers sits on the dressing table, whose scalloped edging in contrasting gingham makes an attractive contrast of pattern with the skirt below, and with the cowslip-coloured lining of the blue curtains beyond. The use of a third colour in the bright pink daisies and the central panel of the quilt (BELOW) accentuates and contrasts with the blue and yellow decorative theme.

An antique quilt with a central panel in a pink floral motif, echoed on the white bed linen, makes a splash of warm colour in the centre of the room. A similar antique quilt could form the starting point for a bedroom colour scheme.

LEFT *A close-up of the window shows how the walls have been edged at skirting height (as at the cornice) with a narrow border of cowslip paint (the secondary colour in the room), and echoed in the yellow reverse to the blue curtains. The three terracotta pots of pansies, in blue and yellow, pick up the theme.*

RIGHT *The wonderfully rich pinkish-blue of this hydrangea makes a vivid colour statement against the similarly toned chambray blue colourwashed wall behind. The play of light and shadow on the flowerheads shows how texture, too, plays its part in our appreciation of colour. The spongewear jug and the simple gingham tablecloth are both classic country-style decorative accessories.*

CHAPTER 6

reds

The use of red in history

OPPOSITE *Swedish style has become immensely popular, helped in part by the recent upsurge in interest in Swedish painters such as Carl Larsson (1853–1919), whose house this is. The wonderful combinations of orange-red with a deep inky blue and natural wood are not typical of the Swedish look but they do have the soft tint of colour that is the hallmark of Swedish interior design. When the room was first painted in the 1890s, the colour scheme did not meet with universal approval, to put it mildly.*

For centuries, red was one of the more expensive pigments for dyes. It has always been considered a regal colour – hence the phrase 'rolling out the red carpet' – and was worn by royalty and heads of state. It was only in the late eighteenth century that synthetic chemical dyes were invented by the Georgians. Suddenly, they had a vivid new palette of colours to work with, and they swept away the muddy tones of the past in a magnificent display of bright, sometimes dazzling, colours. This coincided with a huge revival of interest in the architecture and decoration of Ancient Greece and Rome, and so the designers of the day began to use clear, jewel-bright colours in their decorative schemes. Red was one of these colours, and was especially favoured by Napoleon. The 'Gothick' gallery of Strawberry Hill, in Twickenham, Middlesex, was designed by Horace Walpole in 1776 and features rich red wallpaper which caused a stir when it was first seen.

Along with new shades of red, of course, came new shades of pink. Examples include the powder pink of the rococo style, soft pinks associated with Marie Antoinette, and rose Pompadour, which is a colour made by Madame de Pompadour and seen in Sèvres porcelain. The combination of pale pink and warm, smoky blue was extremely popular in what became known as the Empire style, which was introduced in France in the late eighteenth century. One of the most famous examples of this style was Madame Recamier's bedroom, designed as part of a restoration by Louis-Martin Berthault of the banker Recamier's house. The walls were decorated with rich, violet-blue silk hangings, the bed was draped in white Indian muslin spangled with gold stars, and the paintwork was pale plaster pink and white. The room was visited by everyone interested in the new fashion in decoration. Another example of pink and blue, from roughly the same period, was the pinkish-red and mid-blue design for the music room of the house of the Director of the Royal Opera in Berlin. Deep pinkish-red panels, inset into plaster pink walls, were outlined in pale blue and the recessed alcove within them painted in blue and pink.

It was the Victorians who really popularized the use of red as it is known today. Red dining rooms and drawing rooms, as well as red hallways, were very much in vogue. The range of colours that were available continued to expand as more dyes were invented. Travellers returning from the Grand Tour brought with them such colours as Pompeiian red, and the spread of the British Empire introduced exotic, spicy shades of red and orange. When Queen Victoria was made Empress of India, she had a room at Osborne House filled with her Indian possessions. Known as the Durbar Room, its colour scheme was burnt red and white. Other popular colour schemes, which are still in vogue today, included burgundy mixed with navy and bottle green. The abundance of pretty pink floral prints and chintzes which were produced are still classic decorating textiles.

At its purest, red is one of the strongest colours in the spectrum. It attracts the eye and appears to advance upon you, so it is no accident that it should be the colour used as a warning signal. Primary red is the colour of fire and can have the same attributes – a brilliant, burning intensity. It is hard to be indifferent to red, as bold splashes of primary red are invigorating, dramatic and full of zest. Interestingly, it is the colour that small children seem to identify with most readily, perhaps because it is so visually arresting.

As with all the shades in the spectrum, red changes when it is mixed with other colours and when dark or light tones are added to it. It therefore covers a wonderfully large range of colours: from shell pink and rose to crushed strawberry and plum; from terracotta and plaster pink to crimson, cherry red, magenta, russet and burgundy. Shades of red vary around the world. There are the spicy reds of India, the vermilions of Chinese reds and the scarlets of Japan. Rich crimson is a colour particularly associated with pre-Revolution Russia, of candlelit interiors glowing red and gold while the snow falls outside. In colonial America, reds were deeper and more sombre, and many of the huge clapboard houses of New England were painted in these colours.

Hotter climates have more earthy and muddy shades of spicy red which are mixed with yellow ochres and clay brown. Terracotta, brick and plaster pink are often associated with Italy and come from pigments such as Venetian and sienna red, as well as the terracotta so abundantly used for roof tiles, floors and urns. Plaster pink and brick are the colours of rough plaster and flaking stucco, and of the beautiful pink local stone which is used in decorative detailing on famous Venetian palazzos.

In the United Kingdom, the Victorians introduced a national love of red which became the colour of many classic tourist symbols – including bright red pillar boxes, scarlet telephone boxes and the cherry red double-decker London bus. By the sea and in the countryside, red can be mixed with white to produce pale pinks, and the exteriors of houses and cottages are often washed with these soft shades. One of the most charming British associations with pink is the abundance of plants with pink flowers, such as roses, peonies, carnations and old-fashioned pinks. They and other pink and red flowers have inspired generations of textile designers to produce chintzes, cottons and linens which are abundantly decorated with floral prints.

Of all the colours in the interior decorator's palette, a pure, bright red such as pillar box red is the most difficult to use well. It makes an extremely strong statement, being both intense and vivid in hue, so any decoration scheme in which it is the major colour needs to be thought through carefully, particularly if large quantities of it are being used. For this reason, it is usually best chosen for rooms other than living rooms and is often

OPPOSITE *Red can be difficult to use successfully in interior decoration because it is such a strong and dominant colour. When employed for small rooms which are not used very frequently, such as bathrooms or dining rooms, it comes into its own, especially when the colour is relieved with interesting decorative surface patterning, as shown here.*

most successful in dining rooms, where it creates a glowing atmosphere. The less pure forms of red – Indian reds, muted fuchsia pinks, terracottas and russet – are softer colours and therefore much easier to live with, and will provide a successful colour scheme in almost any room. That said, a strong, pure red can transform a room with less than wonderful proportions into an almost magical environment.

Pure reds

These colours are the primary reds, vermilions and scarlets familiar to us through post office red, tomato red, hunting scarlet and poppy red. When used as a major theme in decoration – as wall colours, for example – they provide the key decorative element to which all other colours play a subsidiary role. In other words, once you have chosen to paint or paper the walls bright red, you have made a commitment which will govern or even dominate all your other colour choices in the room. This is not true of a less demanding colour, such as blue, green or yellow, which will often provide a background to other colours. Red works well with other vivid colours such as yellow and bright green, and is particularly successful with white.

Red and white

The use of white as a contrasting colour to a pure and strong red such as scarlet, vermilion or crimson creates a fresh, appealing and cheerful effect. It will also help to prevent the red from being too overpowering. Red and white gingham, stripes, ticking, country cottons and red and white spotted handkerchiefs – all with their connotations of rustic life – are appealingly clean-looking. They can look good with navy blue, if you want to tone down the brightness, and you can use off-white rather than pure white for a more muted contrast in colour.

Red and white combinations work well for informal rooms, such as kitchens and children's rooms, as well as for bathrooms. The proportions of each colour will affect the overall look – a mainly red room, with touches of white, will be rich, warm and atmospheric, while a mainly white room, with touches of red, will be modern, fresh and uplifting. Red and white can be warmed by the addition of indigo or sunflower yellow.

Red and yellow

Pure forms of red and yellow are sometimes difficult to use together as they can be too dominating, but they are a wonderful combination for a sunny, Provençal or rustic kitchen, or even a child's playroom, when they can evoke the colours of red poppies growing in a field of corn. The combination of red and yellow also works well in the muddier shades of Indian red and yellow ochre. When deep burgundy and pale gold are combined, or rich tomato with old gold, the effect is extremely attractive. Using red as the predominant theme for the walls and the gold as a supporting colour – for details and fabrics, perhaps – has been a major theme in many interiors.

Red and gold

With its connotations of royalty and majesty, a red theme can look sumptuous when combined with rich gold. The combination of red and gold was particularly popular when associated with velvets, brocades and tapestries in both Renaissance interiors and in the Gothic revival of the Victorian and Edwardian periods. These 'royal' colours of red and gold, along with imperial purple, instantly create a feeling of richness, wealth and luxury, and often demand lavish swathes of fabric in detailed patterns. They can also be very successful when combined with deep blue, with cream and with deep green for this Empire or Renaissance style, particularly when teamed with rich fabrics such as damasks, jacquards, velvets, chenilles, silks and brocades.

A red and gold decorating theme can be used for bathrooms as well as for dining rooms and bedrooms. The gold element could be a pattern on fabric; trimmings or finishing details such as gold piping, gilded picture frames and mirrors; or gilded furniture. Small rooms will acquire an almost cocoon-like warmth and intimacy from the use of red, and it is often the ideal solution for a small, cold room which gets little light, as it provides an instant lift of vigour, and creates a warm, glowing atmosphere. Touches of gold will tone down the red.

This marvellously ornate, Gothic room at St Mary's Training College at Twickenham in Surrey proves that a well-chosen red can add depth and warmth to large, open spaces.

Terracotta

This wonderful, rich, warm, brick-like colour can be the most appealing of all the reds, and the easiest to use in decoration since it combines well with a wide range of other colours including gold, yellow, bottle green, cobalt blue and turquoise in shades that vary from light to dark. Terracotta is a dominant feature in decoration all over the world. Based on natural earth and stone colours and the pigments of burnt sienna, light red and Indian red, it varies according to the area in which it is produced and the minerals found locally, so can be browner if burnt umber or sienna is added, or more yellow if yellow ochre is added. In Mexico, a deep, rich, earthy terracotta is painted on the houses, and is often combined with sapphire blue as a direct contrast. Old Italian frescoes feature a wonderfully soft, pinky-gold terracotta, often used with dull gold, olive green and white in colour schemes that are well worth imitating.

In decorating, warm colours, such as plaster pink and brick, represent more subtle shades of terracotta. Brick can be a very smart colour and is a more 'neutral' terracotta colour for downstairs decorating as well as for more masculine bedrooms. A wonderfully warm, redder shade of terracotta is russet, which is especially effective in traditional paisley and furnishing fabrics. Terracotta is one of the oldest forms of ceramic ware. Aged and weathered, it takes on a soft, warm character and its unglazed, undecorated quality has become immensely popular today for tiles and ceramic ware.

Plums and burgundies

Deep, bluish reds, such as plum, cherry, claret and burgundy, have a very distinct character which is determined by the amount of blue added to the red and the darkness of the overall tone. They convey a feeling of autumn and winter, of fireside warmth and evening darkness, and were much used in Victorian times to produce a sense of solidity, security and strength. Dark burgundy, which is the colour of juicy berries, creates a calm, reflective atmosphere and therefore works well in studys and libraries. When combined with navy, dark green, sand or gold, it is excellent for decorating downstairs rooms.

Today, these colours tend to be used in relatively small amounts, and often with one or more contrasting colours to offset the darkness – mustard yellows, mid-greens and turquoises are all good choices. Dusty plum was a popular colour in the Art Deco movement, especially when combined with pea green, and was also much used by William Morris in his textile designs. It enjoyed a big revival in the early 1970s.

Pink

Pink is made from combinations of red and white, sometimes with a little yellow or blue added, and ranges from the palest shell pinks, roses, powder pinks and plaster pinks (which are sometimes almost neutrals because of the paleness of their tone), to the deep, strong pinks such as fuchsia, crushed strawberry, shocking pink, hot pink and raspberry, all of which contain much less white and far more red. Being composed of lots of white, pink is a very fresh colour. It is feminine, pretty and romantic, and is a marvellous colour

for floral prints, from large splashy pink chintzes to simple country sprigs and faded linens. The colours reflect the pink flowers seen in gardens and so bring the garden into the home. For this reason, green is an ideal complement to pink in a decorating scheme because it represents the colour of foliage.

In recent years pink has become an extremely popular colour in the home decorator's repertoire, especially for sitting rooms and bedrooms, and is often combined with another colour such as green or blue, and occasionally yellow. Rose and sapphire form a lovely, pastel combination, with raspberry and kingfisher blue making an effective stronger-toned mixture. Pink has long been popular as a colourway in floral fabrics, such as chintzes, linens and sprigged country cottons, but has recently found a new vogue as a strong decorating colour in its own

right, sometimes teamed with dusty yellow, teal or smoky blue, and used in novel settings such as kitchens. Bright shades of pink are also used as solid blocks of colour mixed with white, chambray blue and apple green.

Muted pinks are some of the easiest colours to live with and they can add a great deal of warmth to a cold-looking room. Pale plaster pink, which is the colour of raw plaster, is a very good 'natural' earthy pink that is muted and less sugary than many pinks. It is a very popular 1990s colour which has been inspired by the interest in neutrals. In Italy and India, dusty, rather faded pinks such as old rose are very popular as a principal decorating colour, often to colourwash both interior and exterior walls.

Hot pink, shocking pink, deep pink and crushed strawberry are also excellent decorating colours, especially when used as an accent colour that brings depth to a pale room. These shades are soft yet full of impact, cheerful and sometimes quirky without being overpowering as primary red can be. They are also good accent colours in multi-coloured floral prints as well as being used plain on upholstered surfaces.

Pink, and especially old rose, is fabulous for a romantic country house style bedroom, with sheer voile drapes and pink chintz fabrics. Pink can look antique and time-worn on tea-stained linens, and soft country tones can be used for a relaxed, yet elegant, drawing room. Pink can be exuberant and arresting in deeper tones for modern, simple schemes with splashes of bright colour for a dramatic, smart downstairs room.

OPPOSITE *This seaside kitchen has been painted in a pale shell pink, which gives it a light and spacious feel. Candy-striped ticking has been used for the simple tab-headed curtains, while a novelty 1950s print provides an element of eccentricity at the smaller window. The kitchen chairs, which are all different, have had their dissimilarity emphasized with an individual, but toning, paint treatment – lichen and ointment pink are among the colours.*

This view of the red dining room from the door demonstrates its richness of contrast, the deep warm ruby red of the walls providing an enclosing cocoon for the central focus – the dining table – with its array of gold-plated china and sparkling crystal. Texture is a key element in this scheme – with the woven fabrics and the walls providing the warmth, contrasted with the sharp brilliance of the gilded cornices, curtain pole and mirror, and the pristine white expanse of the damask tablecloth.

A Red Dining Room

This rich, luxurious dining room uses glowing Indian red to great effect as the major element in the colour scheme. It transforms a functional room into one with a particularly strong character and in which dark colours play the dominant role. Such an obvious colour statement might be too overpowering in a living room or bedroom, but it is possible to do this in a dining room because red is an ideal colour for a special room which is not used everyday, especially if it comes to life at night. When combined with candlelight bouncing off the gilding, glassware and textured walls, red creates a marvellous, glowing atmosphere. Although the architecture of this room, with its high ceilings, lends itself well to this kind of elegant, sophisticated and formal style, this scheme would work equally well in a smaller room.

The essence of this decorative scheme is the colour and texture of the walls, which have been colourwashed in two shades of red. Colourwashing is particularly effective in this context, where different shades of red are used because, instead of the matt finish that a plain colour provides, colourwashed walls reflect light.

An important touch in this room is the antiqued gilding of the cornices, which helps to create the rich look while adding a further glow to the room. Covering the dining table, which forms a large expanse in the centre of the room, is a sparkling white damask cloth which creates a contrast of tone that is further enhanced by the off-white marble of the fireplace surround and the off-white painted ceiling.

Another element that lifts the overall colour scheme and acts as a counterpoint to the deep red because of their light-reflecting qualities is the use of mirrors and glass. The large mirror over the fireplace, with its gilded frame, bounces back reflections from the window, while the chandelier and the glasses on the table also pick up these reflections.

The chenille curtains create a suitably Renaissance feel, partly from the combination of the classic colourway of navy, burgundy and old gold, and partly from the broad stripes. These have been created by stitching panels of the different fabrics together, then emphasizing the seams with braid in the same three colours. This is relatively simple to do, and creates an individual touch to the room. Interlining the curtains with extra-thin wadding gives them the appearance of rich Renaissance wall hangings and the three stripes make them look like beautiful flags. It is worth noting that in designing these striped curtains, the stripes were cut in proportion to the window. These curtains give weight and emphasis to the window, as a contrast to the darkness of the walls. The underblind, made from an elegant woven jacquard in old gold through which the light can pour, also helps to brighten the overall effect.

The dining chairs have also been covered in a woven jacquard in the same colours as

OPPOSITE *Woven pattern is at the heart of this combination, as these chairs upholstered in a gold and burgundy jacquard and the figured damask tablecloth demonstrate. By reversing the fabric treatment on the chairs, using one colourway for the front and another for the chair back and seat, with a contrasting piping, attention is drawn to the pattern of the fabric.*

those used for the curtains, but with a twist. A floral, elegant gold-coloured jacquard has been used for the chair backs, while the seats and reverse of the chairs have been covered in the burgundy colourway, and piped in navy cord. This reflects the three colours used in the curtains. If your dining chairs are not upholstered, you could still copy this idea by making loose covers for them and combining the fabrics in a similar way. The burgundy and gold theme is echoed in the fitted cover for the armchair by the window, which is covered in the same gold jacquard as the chair backs and given a burgundy chenille cushion to create a lavish but elegant and sophisticated atmosphere.

Gilded pole

You can use various methods for gilding, including a very good gilding cream which can be bought in several shades in small pots. It is fairly expensive and if you are gilding a large area, as here, then you will find it less costly to make up your own gilding paint from bronze powder and polyurethane varnish. You can buy the bronze powder at any specialist paint supplier.

you will need Sandpaper • White spirit or rectified turpentine (optional) • Emulsion-based paint in dark maroon • Bronze powder • Polyurethane varnish

1 When gilding a curtain pole, you need to decorate not only the pole itself but also its component parts – the finials and the supports.

2 Sand back the pole to remove any varnish or stain, and then clean the sanded surface with white spirit or rectified turpentine to neutralize it. (If you use one of the newer furniture paints in Step 3 you can omit this step – most of the paints will cover varnished wood, but check the instructions on the can first.)

3 Paint the pole with emulsion-based paint to prime it, ideally in a dark maroon colour. Here, alizarin crimson acrylic paint was mixed with a little Prussian blue acrylic paint to tint an emulsion base, but a deep reddish-brown purpose-bought matt water-based furniture paint or household emulsion will serve the same purpose.

4 Mix a teaspoonful of bronze powder with polyurethane varnish, and then stipple this medium on to the pole with a stiff brush, making sure you do not overload the brush. Aim to create an uneven, mottled finish, so that the base coat shows through. Leave to dry for 24 hours and then give the pole a coat of polyurethane varnish for protection.

LEFT *Deep blue, red and gold are the principal colours of these oriental-inspired antique cups and saucers. Attractive and colourful ceramics can often form the inspiration for a particular colour scheme, which is then expanded to encompass the furnishings in the room.*

RIGHT *Crystal glassware has a special ability to reflect light, while the arrangement of deep red roses and blue anemones in the centre of the table picks up the colour theme of the room. The trailing stems of ivy add a contrast of colour and introduce a note of informality.*

ABOVE *The uneven colour and texture of the paint effect on the walls gives them life and warmth which a flat, uniform colour does not provide. The secret is to apply two or three diluted coats that are tonally similar, giving a depth and density of hue which contrasts beautifully with the gilded cornice.*

RIGHT *Texture plays an important part in the way we perceive colour. Here, the glossiness of the fruit contrasts with the more matt texture of the walls behind, while the glow from the mahogany table matches the sheen on the porcelain dish. The white and blue of the glaze make a dramatic contrast with the deep tones of the red.*

A warm glow suffuses this colonial-inspired bathroom, with its rich and eclectic mixture of colour and texture. The warm terracotta colourwashed and white-stencilled walls are the dominant feature, seconded by the informally draped red checked curtains at the large window. Antique and ethnic furniture takes the place of standard fitted bathroom cabinets, giving this large bathroom an exotic character with a relaxing style.

A Terracotta Bathroom

Conjuring up images of India and the colonial era, this eccentric bathroom has an almost tent-like feel to it – warm, enclosing and secure. Ethnic and colonial chairs and cupboards, informal checked cushions and Indian throws have all been used in this large bathroom to give it an informal, comfortable and quirky character. The old claw-foot bath, and the texture and warmth of the old pine floorboards, give the room a lived-in, familiar quality and retain a sense of 'Englishness' in this exotic decorating scheme.

Touches of white bring the terracotta to life and make it less intense while also picking up the white enamelling from the bath and washbasin. The stencilled pattern on the walls, inspired by Indian wood blocks, has been created in broad stripes, using three different stencils. This is a very successful way of creating an irregular, spontaneous, pattern. The white ceiling and white picture rail help to define and enclose the pattern. The mix of terracotta, turmeric and other spice colours also brings warmth and life to the room because they are not perfectly co-ordinated colours but an eclectic mix of spice colours, so create a relaxed and natural feel.

Generous swathes of brightly coloured Madras check cotton at the windows – in a different, deeper and purer red than that used for the walls – helps to make the bathroom less formal, as does the lack of tiling and other hard surfaces which are so commonly used in bathrooms. The sides of the white enamel bath have been painted in deep red, while the plain white enamel basin has been given a wooden surround, inspired by a seaside windbreak, covered in a strong yellow Madras check.

This style of bathroom, with only minimum attention paid to the function of the room, is ideal for adults, but less suitable for a family bathroom where large quantities of water will probably find their way on to the walls and floor. It would work very well, on a smaller scale, for an en suite bathroom to a master bedroom in which the colours are reversed, with white being the principal colour and Indian red and warm golden browns the secondary colours.

This scheme shows how a bathroom can be far more than a purely functional room, and you can devise a really dramatic scheme. This bathroom is particularly wonderful for displaying the owner's collection of ethnic artefacts collected from faraway travels. A decorative scheme like this would work equally well in a kitchen or dining room.

Plaited rag rug

A simple, plaited rug can be made up from strips of left-over fabric – cottons, wools or whatever you have to hand. However, it is best not to mix the types of fabric in one rug, and it looks nicer if you limit the colour palette to a range of three or four colours, and tones of these colours. Part of the charm of this rug comes from seeing the raw edges of the fabric strips, but if you prefer a smoother, harder-wearing finish, the strips should be cut to twice the width of these and the edges folded in to meet in the centre; the strips are then folded in half. (A proprietary trimming-and-tapemaking tool makes the job easier.)

you will need   Selection of fabrics • Strong thread

1 Tear up strips of fabric into lengths roughly 4 cm (1½ in) wide. Knot three pieces of fabric together at one end and pin the knot to a stable surface. Plait the fabric.

2 When you reach the end of a strip, hand-sew a new strip to it, overlapping the ends. (An even quicker, but less hard-wearing, method is simply to wrap the end of the new strip around the old one.) Continue to plait until the plait is several metres (yards) long.

3 Now begin coiling the plait into a circle, hand-sewing the coils together on the reverse side. (If you are using wider, folded strips, the traditional method is to lace adjacent coils together invisibly.) When you have coiled the entire plait, join on more strips and plait them together, then continue coiling the plait and sewing it together.

4 When the rug is the size you require, taper the strips and oversew the end of the plait to secure it and stop it fraying. Tuck the end under the adjacent coil and sew in place. Neatly sew in the ends of the thread, then trim them so no loose ends are visible.

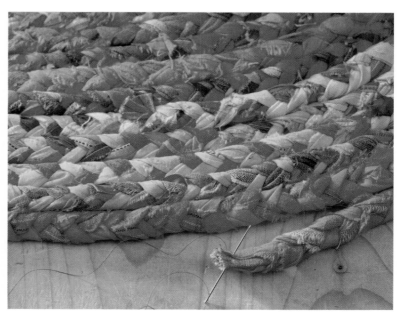

LEFT *The rich colours of the curtain fabric need no further adornment. Simple tie-backs made from a strip of the same fabric keep the curtains in position, while the pattern-mixing theme is taken up in the ethnic quilt thrown over the back of a planter's chair.*

RIGHT *A framed Indian print, the ethnic cupboard and the small wooden box help to create the inspiration for this colonial bathroom. A mixture of freehand painting and stencilling, drawn from Indian wood block designs, has been used to create a repeating sequence of three different stripes on the terracotta-washed walls.*

Laura Ashley Shops

UNITED KINGDOM

LONDON SHOPS

Brent Cross (clothes only)
  0181 202 2679
Chelsea 0171 823 7550
Covent Garden 0171 240 1997
Ealing 0181 579 5197
Kensington 0171 938 3751
Knightsbridge (clothes only)
  0171 823 9700
Knightsbridge (home
  furnishings only)
  0171 235 9797
Marble Arch 0171 355 1363
Oxford Circus 0171 437 9760

COUNTRY SHOPS

Aberdeen 01224 625787
Aylesbury 01296 84574
Banbury 01295 271295
Barnet 0181 449 9866
Bath 01225 460341
Bedford 01234 211416
Belfast 01232 233313
Beverley 01482 872444
Birmingham 0121 631 2842
Bishops Stortford
  01279 655613
Bournemouth (clothes only)
  01202 293764
Brighton 01273 205304
Bristol, Broadmead
  0117 922 1011
Bristol, Clifton 0117 927 7468
Bromley 0181 290 6620
Bury St Edmunds
  01284 755658
Cambridge 01223 351378
Canterbury 01227 450961
Cardiff 01222 340808
Carlisle 01228 48810
Chelmsford 01245 359602
Cheltenham 01242 580770

Chester (clothes only)
  01244 313964
Chester (home furnishings only)
  01244 316403
Chichester 01243 775255
Colchester 01206 562692
Derby 01332 361642
Dudley 01384 79730
Eastbourne 01323 411955
Edinburgh (clothes only)
  0131 225 1218
Edinburgh (home furnishings
  only) 0131 225 1121
Epsom 01372 739595
Exeter 01392 53949
Farnham 01252 712812
Gateshead 0191 493 2411
Glasgow 0141 226 5040
Guildford 01483 34152
Harrogate 01423 526799
Heathrow 0181 759 1951
Hereford 01432 272446
High Wycombe 01494 442394
Hitchin 01462 420445
Horsham 01403 259052
Ipswich 01473 216828
Ipswich 01473 721124
Isle of Man 01624 801213
Jersey 01534 608084
Kings Lynn 01553 768881
Kingston 0181 549 0055
Leamington Spa 01926 314584
Leeds 0113 245 0622
Leicester 01162 513165
Lincoln 01522 511611
Llanidloes 01686 412557
Maidstone 01622 750138
Manchester 0161 834 7335
Middlesbrough 01642 226034
Milton Keynes 01908 660190
Newcastle-Under-Lyme
  01782 662014
Newport I.O.W. 01983 821806

Northampton (clothes only)
  01604 231975
Norwich 01603 632958
Nottingham 01159 503366
Oxford 01865 791689
Perth 01738 623141
Peterborough 01733 311766
Plymouth 01752 268344
Preston 01772 202425
Reading 01734 594313
Richmond 0181 940 9556
Salisbury 01722 338383
Sheffield 0114 270 1855
Sheffield Meadowhall
  0114 256 8221
Shrewsbury 01743 351467
Skipton 01756 700301
Solihull 0121 704 4344
Southampton 01703 228944
Southport 01704 546214
St Albans 01727 864611
Stockport 0161 474 7927
Stratford-Upon-Avon
  01789 298852
Sutton 0181 643 9790
Sutton Coldfield
  0121 355 3671
Swindon 01793 641727
Taunton 01823 288202
Tenterden 01580 765188
Torquay 01803 291443
Truro 01872 223019
Tunbridge Wells 01892 534431
Watford 01923 254411
Wilmslow 01625 535331
Winchester 01962 855716
Windsor (clothes only)
  01753 854345
Windsor (home furnishings
  only) 01753 831456
Worcester 01905 20177
Worthing 01903 205160
Yeovil 01935 79863
York 01904 627707

REPUBLIC OF IRELAND
Cork 00 3532 127 4070
Dublin 00 3531 679 5433

HOMEBASES
Within Sainsbury's Homebase
  House and Garden Centres
Basildon 01268 584088
Basingstoke 01256 469510
Bath 01225 339293
Blackheath 0181 856 9767
Bradford 01274 611929
Branksome 01202 768311
Brentford 0181 847 2214
Camberley 01276 686227
Cardiff 01222 499675
Catford 0181 461 0606
Chelmsford 01245 257257
Chichester 01243 533373
Colchester 01206 869187
Coventry 01203 715901
Crawley 01293 538351
Crayford 01322 558614
Croydon 0181 684 8250
Derby 01332 291260
Enfield 0181 366 2236
Gloucester 01452 526806
Guildford 01483 304115
Harlow 01279 413355
Hatfield 01707 275837
Hendon 0181 200 7737
Hull 01482 572434
Ilford 0181 590 0212
Ipswich 01473 721124
Kensington 0171 603 2285
Kingston 0181 949 7861
Leeds 0113 268 5010
Leicester 0116 254 6075
Luton 0582 593445
Maidstone 01622 715400
Mill Hill 0181 203 7740
Milton Keynes 01908 692727
New Southgate 0181 368 1698

Newcastle-Under-Lyme
  01782 711752
Northampton 01604 234143
Norwich 01603 417474
Nottingham 0115 941 3885
Oldbury 0121 544 7333
Orpington 01689 890353
Oxford 01865 747979
Penge 0181 778 4214
Rayleigh Weir 01268 745374
Reading 01734 584572
Richmond 0181 876 2235
Rochester 01634 200088
Romford 01708 730326
Sheffield 0174 255 5175
Southampton 01703 510098
Stockport 1061 474 7489
Swansea 01792 650935
Swindon 01793 487125
Tunbridge Wells 01892 546646
Wakefield 01924 387011
Walsall 01922 29524
Walsgrave 01203 602086
Waltham Cross 01992 625275
Walthamstow 0181 531 8233
Watford 01923 252075
Willesden 0181 459 3989
Wimbledon 0181 946 9802
Worcester 01905 420401
Worle 01934 512628
York 01904 643911

UNITED STATES OF AMERICA
Albany 518 452 4998
Ann Arbor 313 747 6620
Ardmore 610 896 0208
Arlington 703 415 2111
Atlanta-Lenox 404 231 0685
Atlanta-Perimeter
  404 395 6027
Austin 512 451 4036
Bal Harbor 305 864 5628
Beachwood 216 831 7621

Birch Run 517 624 9297
Birmingham 205 985 0090
Bluffton 803 837 4339
Boca Raton 407 368 5622
Boston 617 536 0505
Bridgewater 908 725 3700
Buffalo 716 681 8600
Burlington/Boston
  617 272 4540
Burlington/Vermont
  802 658 5006
Carmel-by-the-Sea
  408 624 8095
Central Valley 914 928 4561
Charleston 803 723 3967
Charlotte 704 362 0926
Charlottesville 804 971 7707
Chattanooga 615 855 5496
Chestnut Hill 617 965 7640
Chicago 312 951 8004
Cincinnati 513 793 5535
Columbus 614 224 5057
Corte Madera 415 924 5770
Costa Mesa 714 545 9322
Cranston 401 946 1211
Dallas-Galleria 214 980 9858
Danbury 203 790 5068
Dayton 513 299 9007
Denver-Cherry Creek
  303 322 9401
Des Moines 515 243 8881
Destin 904 654 9771
Edina 612 920 2811
Fairfax 703 352 7960
Farmington 203 521 8967
Fort Lauderdale 305 563 2300
Fort Worth 817 346 4666
Freeport 207 865 3300
Germantown 901 756 7036
Gilroy 408 848 5470
Glendale 818 242 0428
Grand Rapids 616 942 6828
Greenville 302 575 1653
Greenwich 203 661 5678

Grosse Pointe 313 886 6960
Hackensack 201 488 0130
Hingham 617 740 4122
Honolulu 808 942 5200
Houston 713 871 9669
Houston/West Oaks
  713 558 6113
Indianapolis 317 848 9855
Jacksonville 904 358 7548
Jeffersonville 614 948 2019
Kansas City 816 931 0731
King of Prussia 610 354 9130
Knoxville 615 558 6385
Lake Forest 708 615 1405
Lancaster 717 397 7116
Lexington 606 253 1724
Little Rock 501 666 0272
Los Angeles 310 553 0807
Louisville 502 585 2424
Manhasset 516 365 4634
McLean 703 827 0074
Miami 305 233 8911
Milwaukee 414 347 1930
Minnetonka 612 546 4613
Montgomery 205 284 7011
Myrtle Beach 803 236 4244
Nashville 615 383 0131
New Haven 203 782 9436
New Orleans 504 522 9403
New York City/Westside
  212 496 5110
New York City/57th Street
  212 752 7300
Newport 401 846 6980
North Bethesda 301 984 3223
Northbrook 708 480 1660
Novi 313 348 9260
Oakbrook 708 572 9195
Oklahoma City 405 848 6252
Omaha 402 390 2085
Orlando 407 351 2785
Osage Beach 314 348 1333
Owings Mills 410 363 2455
Palm Beach 407 832 3188

Palm Beach Gardens
  407 624 5901
Palm Springs 619 322 2099
Palo Alto 415 328 0560
Phoenix 602 956 6043
Pittsburgh 412 367 8881
Pittsburgh 412 621 0735
Pleasanton 510 463 8714
Portland 503 224 0703
Prince William 703 474 3124
Princeton 609 683 4760
Raleigh 919 781 1076
Reading 215 373 5495
Redondo Beach 310 542 4436
Richmond 804 740 1406
Ridgeland 601 957 9063
Rochester 507 287 1073
Sacramento 916 923 5696
Salt Lake City 801 363 8408
San Antonio 512 377 2833
San Diego 619 234 0663
San Diego 619 452 6116
San Francisco 415 788 0190
San Marcos 512 396 5570
Santa Ana 714 834 1211
Santa Barbara 805 682 8878
Santa Clara 408 244 3551
Scarsdale 510 947 5920
Schaumberg 708 619 9110
Seattle 206 343 9637
Secausus 201 863 3066
Short Hills 201 467 5657
Skokie 708 673 6604
Southampton 516 287 2104
Stamford 203 324 1067
Stony Brook 516 689 6622
St Augustine 904 823 9533
St Louis 314 993 4410
Tampa 813 253 2177
Towson 410 825 0362
Troy 810 649 0890
Tulsa 918 749 5001
Walnut Creek 510 947 5920
Washington 202 338 5481

Westport 203 226 7495
Williamsburg 804 229 0353
Williamsburg 319 668 1555
Winston Salem 919 760 3733
Winter Park 407 740 8900
Woodbury 516 367 2810
Woodland Hills 818 346 7560
Worthington 614 433 9011

MOTHER AND CHILD
  STORES
Birmingham 205 987 7566
Chestnut Hill 617 965 5687
Denver-Cherry Creek
  303 322 9403
Farmington-Hartford
  203 561 4870
Hackensack-Riverside
  201 342 1222
Houston 713 622 2262
Kansas City 816 931 2810
King of Prussia 610 354 9137
Princeton 609 683 1300
Redondo Beach 310 542 6228
Schaumberg 708 240 1910
Short Hills 201 467 5657
Stamford 203 359 9902
Tulsa 918 749 5063
Walnut Creek 510 947 3932

HOME FURNISHING
  STORES
Alexandria 703 739 2144
Ardmore 215 896 8293
Atlanta 404 842 0102
Boston 617 357 5151
Burlingame 415 344 1774
Costa Mesa 714 545 7927
Dallas 214 691 6871
Kansas City 816 531 8971
New York City 212 735 5000
Ridgewood 201 670 0868
Short Hills 201 564 9600
Washington 202 686 1200

CANADA
Willowdale 416 223 9507
Calgary, Alberta 403 269 4090
London, Ontario 519 434 1703
Montreal 514 284 9225
Ottawa 613 238 4882
Quebec 418 659 6660
Sherway Gardens, Etobicoke
  416 620 7222
Toronto 416 922 7761
Toronto-Yorkdale
  416 256 2040
Vancouver 604 688 8729
Winnipeg 204 943 3093

AUSTRIA
Graz 0316 844398
Innsbruck
  0152 579254/579257
Linz 070 797700
Salzburg 0662 840344
Vienna 01 5129312

BELGIUM
Antwerp 03 2343461
Bruges 050 349059
Brussels (clothes only)
  02 5112813
Brussels (home furnishings
  only) 02 5120447
Gent 092 240819

FRANCE
Paris
94 rue de Rennes 1 45 48 43 89
95 rue de Raymond Poincaré
  1 45 01 24 73
261 rue Saint Honoré
  1 42 86 84 13
Galeries Lafayette, 40 bld
  Haussmann
  second floor (clothes only)
  1 42 82 34 56
  fifth floor (home furnishings

only) 1 42 82 04 11
Au Printemps, 64 bld
  Haussmann
  second floor (clothes only)
  1 42 82 52 10
  seventh floor (home
  furnishings only)
  1 42 82 44 20
Au Printemps, Centre
  Commercial Vélizy
  Avenue de l'Europe, Vélizy,
  Villacoublay
  Niveau 2 (clothes and home
  furnishings) 1 30 70 87 66
Au Printemps, Centre
  Commercial Parly 2
  Avenue Charles de Gaulle, Le
  Chesnay
  Niveau 1 (home furnishings
  only) 1 39 54 22 44
  Niveau 2 (clothes only)
  1 39 54 22 44
Aix-en-Provence 42 27 31 92
Bordeaux 56 44 10 30
Clemont-Ferrand 73 31 22 05
Dijon 80 30 04 44
Lille 20 06 90 06
Lyon 78 37 18 19
Montpelier 67 60 75 75
Nancy 83 35 21 09
Nantes 40 73 17 18
Nice 93 16 06 93
Rouen 35 70 20 02
Strasbourg 88 75 18 90
Toulon 94 21 89 58
Toulouse 61 21 38 85

GERMANY
Augsburg 0821 154021
Berlin (home furnishings only)
  030 8826201
Berlin (clothes only)
  030 8824934

Berlin (Kadewe) 030 2183016
Bielefeld 0521 177188
Bonn 0228 654908
Bremen 0421 170443
Cologne 0221 2580470
Dortmund 0231 141009
Düsseldorf 0211 8648732
Essen 0201 200482
Frankfurt 069 288791
Hamburg 040 371173
Hanover 0511 326919
Heidelberg 06 22 1189851
Karlsruhe 0721 25968
Munich 089 2608224
Münster 0251 42272
Nuremberg 0911 24518
Stuttgart 0711 2261064
Wiesbaden 0611 302086

ITALY
Milan 2 86463532

LUXEMBOURG
Luxembourg 221 320

NETHERLANDS
Amsterdam 020 6228087
Arnhem
  085 430250 (026 4430250)
Eindhoven 040 (2)435022
Groningen 050 (3)185060
The Hague 070 3600540
Maastricht 043 (3)250972
Rotterdam 010 4148535
Utrecht 030 (2)313051

SPAIN
Barcelona 341 25490

SWITZERLAND
Basel 061 2619757
Bern 031 3120696
Geneva (clothes only)
  22 33113494

Geneva (home furnishings only)
  22 33103048
Zurich 01 2211394

ASIA
HONG KONG SHOPS IN
SHOPS
Seibu 852 2801 7849
Sogo 852 2891 1787

JAPAN
Ginza 03 3571 5011
Yagoto 052 836 7086
Kichijoji 0422 21 1203
Jiyugaoka 03 3724 0051
Yokohama LMP 045 222 5308
Shibuya 03 3464 5011
Futako Tamagawa
  03 3708 3151
Gifu Melsa 0582 66 3136
Fukuoka Tenjin 092 716 7415

JAPAN SHOPS IN SHOPS
TOKYO
Mitsukoshi Nihonbashi
  03 3241 5617
Mitsukoshi Ikebukuro
  03 3987 6074
Tokyu 03 3477 3836
Keio Shinjuku 03 3344 0080
Mitsukoshi Ginza 03 3561 4050
Tobu Ikebukuro 03 3980 0041

REST OF JAPAN
Mitsukoshi Yokohama
  045 323 1683
Saikaya Kawasaki
  0044 211 8581
Saikaya Yokosuka
  0468 23 1234
Chiba Mitsukoshi 043 227 4731
Mitsukoshi Bandai
  025 243 6333
Sapporo Tokyu 011 212 2658

Kintetsu Abeno 06 625 2332
Hankyu Umeda 06 365 0793
Kawanishi Hankyu
  0727 56 1622
Mitsukoshi Hiroshima
  082 241 5055
Hiroshima Sogo 082 225 2955
Hakata Izutsuya 092 452 2181
Fukuoka Tamaya 092 271 6588
Nagoya Mitsukoshi
  052 252 1838
Matsuzakaya Nagoyacki
  052 565 4339
Seishin Sogo 078 992 1586
Kobe Ilankyu 078 360 7528
Daimaru Kobe 078 333 4079
Tama Sogo 0423 39 2450
Kintetsu Kyoto
  075 365 8024/8013
Be Me Machida Daimaru
  0427 24 8174
Sanyo Himeji 0792 23 4792
Tenmaya Fukuyama
  0849 27 2214
Mitsukoshi Matsuyama
  0899 46 4829
Saikaya Fujisawa 0466 27 1111
Matsuzukaya Yokkaichi
  0593 551241
Cita Tokiwa 0975 33 1741
Bon Belta Narita 0476 23 3236
Hanamatsu Matsubishi
  053 452 2941
Kagoshima Mitsukoshi
  0992 39 4635
Saga Tamaya 0952 28 0608
Kintetsu Nara 0742 30 2751
Kokura Izutsuya 093 522 2627

SINGAPORE
SHOPS IN SHOPS
Sogo 65 334 1014
Isetan Scotts 65 735 0495

TAIWAN
SHOPS IN SHOPS
Ta-Lee Isetan 886 7 241 8860
Pacific Sogo 886 2 740 9662
Shin Kong Mitsukoshi
  886 2 382 4859

Stockists and Suppliers

UNITED KINGDOM

FABRICS AND TEXTILES

The Blue Door
77 Church Road
London SW13 9HH
0181 748 9785

Colefax and Fowler
118 Garratt Lane
London SW18 4DJ
0181 874 6484
Chintz fabrics

The Conran Shop
Michelin House
81 Fulham Road
London SW3 6RB
0171 589 7401
For fabrics

George Weil
Showroom
18 Hanson Street
London W1P 7DB
0171 580 3763

Mail order
Reading Arch Road
Redhill
Surrey RH1 1H6
For dyes, fabric paints and fabrics

Hess and Co
7 Warple Mews
Warple Way
London W3 0RS
0181 746 1366
For interlinings and linings

John Lewis Partnership plc
Oxford Street
London W1Z 1EX
0171 629 7711
Excellent haberdashery and lighting departments; branches nationwide

Ian Mankin
109 Regent's Park Road
London NW1 8UR
0171 722 0997
For fabrics

Just Fabrics
Burford Antique Centre
Cheltenham Road
Burford
Oxfordshire OX8 4JA
01993 823391
Plain-coloured chintzes and other fabrics

Liberty
210–220 Regent Street
London W1R 6AH
0171 734 1234
Plain and patterned cotton fabrics, silks and linens

The Natural Fabric Company
Wessex Place
127 High Street
Hungerford
Berkshire RG17 0DL
01468 684002

VV Rouleaux
10 Symons Street
Sloane Square
London SW3 2TJ
0171 730 3125
For an exceptional selection of ribbons, braids, cords, tassels and other trimmings

Sanderson
112–120 Brompton Road
London SW3 1JJ
0171 584 3344
Fabrics, William Morris prints, furniture

PAINTS AND PAPERS

J. W. Bollom
13 Theobald's Road
London WC1X 8FN
0171 242 0313
General painting supplies
314 Old Brompton Road
London SW5 9JH
(Showroom)

C. Brewer
327 Putney Bridge Road
London SW15 2PG
0181 788 9335
General painting supplies. Various branches in S. E. England

Brodie and Middleton Ltd
68 Drury Lane
London WC2B 5SP
0171 836 3289
Pigments and paints

Cornelissen and Son Ltd
105 Great Russell Street
London WC1B 3RY
0171 636 1045
Pigments and brushes

Craig & Rose plc
172 Leith Walk
Edinburgh EH6 5ER
0131 554 1131
Glazes, specialist brushes. Stockists nationwide.

Daler-Rowney Ltd
PO Box 10
Southern Industrial Estate
Bracknell
Berkshire RG12 8ST
01344 424621
Artists' materials

The English Stamp Company
Sunnydown
Worth Matravers
Dorset BH19 3JP
01929 439117

Farrow & Ball
Uddens Trading Estate
Wimbourne
Dorset BH21 7NL
01202 876141
*National Trust range of
historical paints*

Foxell & James Ltd
57 Farringdon Road
London EC1M 3JH
0171 405 0152
*Varnishes, primers, paints,
glazes, floor finishes, rabbit-skin
glue, whiting, metal powders*

Green & Stone
259 Kings Road
London SW3 5EL
0171 352 0837
Artists' materials

W. Habberley Meadows Ltd
5 Saxon Way
Chelmsley Wood
Birmingham B37 5AY
0121 770 2905
*Artists' paints and brushes,
gilding materials*

J. T. Keep & Co.
13 Theobalds Road
London WC1X 8SN
0171 242 7578
General decorating suppliers

Lyn Le Grice Stencil Design Ltd
The Stencil House
53 Chapel Street
Penzanze
Cornwall TR18 4AS
01736 64193
Stencil books, kits and materials

John Myland
80 Norwood High Street
London SE27 9NW
0181 670 9161
Artists' brushes and materials

Paint Magic
116 Sheen Road
Richmond
Surrey TW9 1UR
0181 940 5503
*Paint effect kits, colourwash,
woodwash, crackle-glaze,
stencilling supplies*

The Paint Service Co. Ltd
19 Eccleston Street
London SW1W 9LX
0171 730 6408

Papers and Paints
4 Park Walk
London SW10 0AD
0171 352 8626

Pavilion Stencils
6a Howe Street
Edinburgh EH3 6TD
0131 225 3590
Stencilling supplies

E. Ploton Ltd
273 Archway Road
London N6 5AA
0181 348 0315
*Metallic powders, gilding
materials*

Potmolen Paint
27 Woodstock Industrial Estate
Warminster
Wiltshire BA12 9DX
01985 213960
*Paints and finishes suitable for
old buildings*

J. H. Ratcliffe & Co. (Paints) Ltd
135a Linaker Street
Southport PR8 5DF
01704 537999
Transparent oil glaze

The Shaker Shop
25 Harcourt Street
London W1H 1DT
0171 724 7672
Old Village buttermilk paints

Stuart R. Stevenson
68 Clerkenwell Road
London EC1M 5QA
0171 253 1693
Gilding materials

UNITED STATES

FABRICS AND TEXTILES
ABC Carpet & Home
888 Broadway
New York
NY 10003
212 473 3000

André Bon
979 Third Avenue
New York
NY 10022
212 355 4012

Clarence House
979 Third Avenue
New York
NY 10022
212 753 2890

Liberty of London
108 West 39th Street
New York
NY 10018
212 391 2150

Pierre Deux Fabrics
870 Madison Avenue
New York
NY 10021
212 570 9343

Scalamandre
950 Third Avenue
New York
NY 10022
212 980 3888

J Schumacher & Company
79 Madison Avenue
New York
NY 10016
212 213 7900

Standard Trimming Co.
306 East 62nd Street
New York
NY 10021
212 355 4012

PAINTS AND PAPERS
Decorating Centers
1555 Third Avenue
New York
NY 10028
212 289 6300

2475 Broadway
New York
NY 10025
212 769 1440

Sam Flax
12 West 20th Street
New York
NY 10011
212 620 3038
425 Park Avenue
New York
NY 10022
212 620 3060

Liberty Paint Co.
969 Columbia Street
Hudson
NY 12534
518 828 4060

Pearl Paint Co.
308 Canal Street
New York
NY 10013
212 431 7932

Wolf Paint and Paper
Janovic Plaza
771 Ninth Avenue
New York
NY 10019
212 245 3241

Janovic Plaza
1150 Third Avenue
New York
NY 10022
212 772 1400

Acknowledgements

The publishers would like to thank the following people for their invaluable help in the production of this book: Mary Batten for her advice and support; Jemima Dyson for her styling and editorial assistance; Chris Churchley for her help; Petra Boase for designing the appliqué tablecloth (pages 156–7) and the plaited rag rug (pages 196–7); Clement Barbic for decorating the red dining room (pages 182–91) and the terracotta bathroom (192–9); Derek Sutton for his help in decorating the other rooms.

Joss Graham Oriental Textiles
10 Eccleston Street
London SW1W 9LT
0171 730 4370

HRW Antiques
4a Kings Avenue
London SW4
0171 978 1026

Graham and Green
4, 7 & 10 Elgin Crescent
London W11 2JA
0171 727 4594

Perez Antique Carpets Gallery
150 Wandworth Bridge Road
London SW6 2LH
0171 589 2199

David Wainwright
251 Portobello Road
London W11
0171 792 1988

The Dining Room Shop
62–4 White Hart Lane
London SW13
0181 878 1020

Ian Mankin
109 Regents Park Road
London NW1 8UR
0171 722 0997

Homeline
33 Parkway
London NW1
0171 485 0744

Harwood Antiques
24 Lower Richmond Road
London SW15 1JP
0181 788 7444

Gallery of Antique Costumes and Textiles
2 Church Street
London NW8
0171 723 9981

Thomas Goode
19 South Audley Street
London W1Y 6BN
0171 499 2823

The Barnes Gallery
51 Church Road
London SW13 9HH
0181 741 1277

Tulissio de Beaumont
Decorative Antiques
277 Lillie Road
London SW6 7PN
0171 385 0156

Farrow and Ball Paint Suppliers
Uddens Trading Estate
Wimborne
Dorset
BH21 7NL
01202 876141

The publishers would like to thank the following companies for permission to reproduce photographs in this book:
8–9 The Laura Ashley Archive; 10 top left Richard Bryant/Arcaid; 10 top right Jacqui Hurst; 10 left of centre The Laura Ashley Archive; 10 bottom left Simon Upton/Robert Harding Picture Library; 10 bottom right Anne Hyde; 11 top left Anne Hyde; 11 top right Anne Hyde; 11 left of centre Rupert Horrox; 11 bottom left Andrew Payne/Belle/Arcaid; 11 bottom right Anne Hyde; 13 The Laura Ashley Archive; 15 Anne Hyde; 17 Richard Waite/Arcaid. designer Louise Cotier; 18 Simon Brown/Robert Harding Picture Library; 19 Andreas von Einsiedel/Robert Harding Picture Library; 23 The Laura Ashley Archive; 24 Geoff Lung/Belle/Arcaid; 25 Robert Harding Picture Library; 39 Richard Bryant/Arcaid, by kind permission of The Mount Vernon Ladies' Association of the Union; 40 National Trust Photographic Library/Bill Batten; 41 The Laura Ashley Archive; 42 Richard Bryant/Arcaid; 50 top left Jacqui Hurst; 50 top right Rupert Horrox; 50 left of centre Jacqui Hurst; 50 right of centre Jacqui Hurst; 50 bottom left Rupert Horrox; 50 bottom right Anne Hyde; 51 top right Lucinda Lambton/Arcaid; 51 left of centre Anne Hyde; 51 bottom left Rupert Horrox; 52 National Trust Photographic Library/Rupert Truman; 55 Richard Bryant/Arcaid; 56 The Laura Ashley Archive; 59 Jan Baldwin/Robert Harding Picture Library; 61 The Laura Ashley Archive; 80 top right Anne Hyde; 80 left of centre Lucinda Lambton/Arcaid; 80 right of centre National Trust Photographic Library/Andreas von Einsiedel; 80 bottom left Jacqui Hurst; 80 bottom right Jacqui Hurst; 81 top right Richard Bryant/Arcaid; 81 left of centre Anne Hyde; 81 bottom left Polly Wreford/Robert Harding Picture Library; 81 bottom right Anne Hyde; 83 Richard Bryant/Arcaid; 85 Fritz von der Schulenburg/Robert Harding Picture Library; 86 Andreas von Einsiedel/Robert Harding Picture Library; 87 Andreas von Einsiedel/Robert Harding Picture Library; 88 The Laura Ashley Archive; 108 top left Anne Hyde; 108 top right Jacqui Hurst; 108 left of centre The Laura Ashley Archive; 108 right of centre The Laura Ashley Archive; 108 bottom left National Trust Photographic Library/Nick Meers; 108 bottom right David Fowler/Arcaid; 109 top right National Trust Photographic Library/Andreas von Einsiedel; 109 left of centre Simon Page-Ritchie/Robert Harding Picture Library; 109 bottom left Mark Fiennes/Arcaid; 109 bottom right Anne Hyde; 113 The Laura Ashley Archive; 114 Richard Bryant/Arcaid; 116 National Trust Photographic Library/Andreas von Einsiedel; 138 top left Anne Hyde; 138 top right Robert O'Dea/Arcaid; 138 bottom left Jacqui Hurst; 138 bottom right Anne Hyde; 138 left of centre Lucinda Lambton/Arcaid; 138 right of centre Robert Harding Picture Library; 139 top left Anne Hyde; 139 left of centre Christopher Drake/Robert Harding Picture Library; 139 bottom left Anne Hyde; 139 bottom left Jacqui Hurst; 143 Jacqui Hurst; 145 The Laura Ashley Archive; 147 The Laura Ashley Archive; 149 Annet Held/Arcaid; 151 Farrell Grehan/Arcaid; 172 top left Trevor Wood/Robert Harding Picture Library; 172 right of centre Christopher Drake/Robert Harding Picture Library; 172 bottom left Tom Leighton/Robert Harding Picture Library; 172 bottom right Walter Rawlings/Robert Harding Picture Library; 173 top left 173 top right Debbie Patterson/Robert Harding Picture Library; 173 left of centre Jan Baldwin/Robert Harding Picture Library; 173 bottom left Jacqui Hurst; 173 bottom right Chrisopher Drake/Robert Harding Picture Library; 175 Richard Bryant/Arcaid; 177 Richard Waite/Arcaid, designer Louise Cotier; 179 David Churchill/Arcaid; 181 The Laura Ashley Archive.

Index